Street Drugs

LOU SAVELLI

43-08 162nd Street • Flushing, NY 11358
www.LooseleafLaw.com • 800-647-5547

©2008 Looseleaf Law Publications, Inc.
All Rights Reserved. Printed in U.S.A.

10-Digit ISBN 1-932777-34-2
13-Digit ISBN 978-1-932777-34-5

No portion of this book may be reproduced without the prior permission of Homefront Protective Group or the author, Lou Savelli. Pocketguide is a trademark of Homefront Protective Group and the Pocketguide Series.

This publication is not intended to replace, nor be a substitute for, any official procedural material issued by your agency of employment or other official source. Looseleaf Law Publications, Inc., the author and any associated advisors have made all possible efforts to ensure the accuracy and thoroughness of the information provided herein but accept no liability whatsoever for injury, legal action or other adverse results following the application or adoption of the information contained in this book.

Cover design by *Sans Serif, Inc.* Saline, Michigan

*Special thanks to Mick Mollica,
an international drug expert,
for providing many of the photos in this book.*

About the Pocketguide Series

Law Enforcement Officers (LEOs) are faced with ever-changing trends and issues and have little time to spend on in-depth research and reference. The Pocketguide series of books have been created to assist law enforcement officers in the endeavor to remain up-to-date on these ever-changing trends. The Pocketguide series provides to the point reference information on contemporary important issues. We at Homefront Protective Group, creators of the Pocketguide series, have painstakingly researched and developed the following valuable and useful information.

The Pocketguide books, as you will see, will provide a current, quick and easy-to- use, pocket-sized tool that was written in an easy to read style. When hundreds of pages of information or volumes of material are not feasible to carry around and time does not permit its study, the Pocketguide books will fill that void and provide the right reference.

Please enjoy this useful pocket-sized book and keep in mind that we wish you safety and efficiency in your endeavor to fight the scourge of crime in our society.

Other Pocketguides now available:

War on Terror
Basic Crime Scene Investigation
Gangs and Their Symbols
Identity Theft Understanding
Graffiti
The Best Cops Jokes Ever
Practical Spanish for Police

Call Toll-Free for other Recent Editions to the Pocketguide Series and a ***Free*** catalog.

(800) 647-5547
Looseleaf Law Publications, Inc.
Flushing, NY

Table of Contents

About the Author v

Why did the author write this book? ix

Drugs, Crime and the U.S. 1

Controlled Substances Act 3

How to Use this Pocketguide 7

Street Drugs 9
    Cocaine 10
    Crack Cocaine 15
    Heroin 20
    Marijuana 25
    Methylamphetamine 33
    PCP (Phencyclidine) aka Angel Dust 41
    Club Drugs 45
    Ecstasy (MDMA) 46
    LSD 52
    2C-B (Nexus) 56

Predatory Drugs 67
    GHB 68
    Ketamine 73

Rohypnol	77
Soma	80

Inhalants	84

Prescription Drugs	87
Narcotics/Opioids/Pain Relievers	89
Depressants	91
Stimulants	93

Anabolic Steroids	94

Plant Drugs	96
Salvia Divinorum	96
Khat	98
Mushrooms	100
Peyote	103

Over the Counter Drugs	104

Bibliography	107

Glossary	108

Field Testing Made Easier with IDenta Drug and Explosive ID Kits	119

About the Author

Lou Savelli, who has spent **all** of his 25 years in law enforcement in the streets, is one of the most decorated officers in NYPD history. He has received over 100 medals for bravery, outstanding police work, life saving rescues, and record-setting investigations. He was chosen as one of the **top 10 of NYPD's most effective leaders of all ranks** (out of nearly 20,000 qualified supervisors in NYPD) and the first supervisor featured in NYPD's Leadership Training School Newsletter because of his innovation and success in the field of leadership and crime fighting.

As the author of nine law enforcement books, he created NYPD's first citywide gang unit called CAGE (Citywide Anti Gang Enforcement) which was awarded the National Gang Crime Research Center's award for **The Most Effective Gang Unit in the U.S.** He has received awards from the FBI, DEA, ATF, Dept of Treasury, U.S. Attorney's Office, Department of State, Los Angeles Sheriff's Department, Canadian law enforcement agencies, Caribbean Law Enforcement Agencies, Italian Government, New South Wales Australia, New Zealand, Mexico, Japan, and many other law enforcement agencies, government agencies and community groups. As a detective, he and his unit were responsible for the **World's Largest Cash Seizure in a Drug Case** ($20 Million) which still holds as a record to this date.

While much of Lou Savelli's investigations are still confidential, he is an internationally-sought after trainer on gangs, youth at risk, terrorism, narcotics investigations, street tactics, drug smuggling, and crime fighting. He has personally lectured before countless audiences, in law enforcement and the private sector, in three countries. He has been frequently quoted in major periodicals such as the *LA Times*, *New York Times*, *New York Newsday*, *New York Daily News*, *Nottingham Press* (United Kingdom), television news reports, many local newspapers across the U.S. and has had his investigations featured in **Time Magazine**, **Newsweek**, **Top Cops TV Series**, **Law Enforcement Technology Magazine**, **American Police Beat Magazine** and other periodicals. Lou Savelli has consulted on such television shows as **Third Watch** (NBC) and *One Life to Live* (ABC) and provided intricate authentic information to television shows such as New York Undercover. He can be seen on the Good Life Network in the documentary series **Homefront America** which examines Homeland Security in the United States today.

As the author of five law enforcement books, several true crime short stories, and numerous articles relating to issues such as terrorism, gangs, criminal investigation, identity theft, and crime prevention, Lou Savelli is a frequent consultant to hundreds of law enforcement officers, throughout the United States and abroad, seeking advice on how to successfully identify and fight crime in their own cities. Lou Savelli has worked extensively with youth at risk, gang members and has conducted educational and motivational speeches for counselors involved in youth and drug counseling.

Lou Savelli is the cofounder and Deputy Director of the East Coast Gang Investigators Assn, a member of the International Counter Terrorism Officers Assn, Midwest Gang Investigators Assn, Oklahoma Gang Investigators Assn, Florida Gang Investigators Assn, International Latino Gang Investigators Assn, International Outlaw Motorcycle Gang Investigators Assn, California Gang Investigators Association, Ontario National Gang Investigators Assn, Southeast Connecticut Gang Activities Group, GANGINFO Network, National Assn of Bunco Investigators, International Association of Identification, Roadwarrior Interdiction Network, and several others. He is a long standing member of several fraternal and law enforcement support associations such as National Police Defense Foundation, Fraternal Order of Police, and International Police Association. Lou Savelli currently holds membership in law enforcement and security professional associations, to wit: International Association of Chiefs of Police (IACP), American Academy for Professional Law Enforcement (AAPLE), and American Society of Industrial Security (ASIS).

His carefully chosen law enforcement instructors provide several training courses each year for the Northeast Counterdrug Training Center, Midwest Counterdrug Training Center, Regional Counterdrug Training Center, RISS

Networks, and many other training academies throughout the United States. Lou Savelli and his instructors have been extremely successful in providing state of the art 'Reality' training to small and rural agencies, as well as larger law enforcement agencies.

He recently retired as the Detective Squad Commander of the NYPD Terrorism Interdiction Unit, which is a pro-active counter-terrorism unit aggressively targeting al-Qaeda and other foreign terrorist groups in the United States. He is a veteran of the rescue and recovery effort at the World Trade Center resulting from the attacks on 9-11-01.

Lou Savelli is a police instructor at the Northeast Counterdrug Training Center in Pennsylvania (www.counterdrug.org), the Midwest Counterdrug Training Center in Iowa (www.counterdrugtraining.org), and the Regional Counterdrug Training Center in Mississippi (www.rcta.org).

Lou Savelli, who has authored several other law enforcement books, written many published short stories, and numerous articles, is also the Chief Executive Officer of Homefront Protective Group (www.homefrontprotect.com), a Law Enforcement Consulting and Training company. He is also the President of a New York based Private Investigation and Security Firm called Homefront Security (www.homefrontsecurity.com).

Why did the author write this book?

Lou Savelli spent several years in the NYPD Narcotics Division, conducting countless "Buy and Bust," street interdiction, undercover operations and even buying drugs himself as an undercover officer in some of New York's most dangerous and drug infested streets. He was later assigned to the New York Drug Enforcement Task Force (NYDETF) which consisted of NYPD Detectives, DEA Special Agents and New York State Police Investigators. During his time with the NYDETF, Lou and his fellow investigators achieved some of the most successful drug cases in the history of law enforcement including the world's largest seizure of drug money (to this date) when they seized $20 Million (See photo below) in a raid from 11 armed Colombian drug dealers operating in New York City.

As a drug investigator and later a supervisor for a long time in the NYPD Gang Unit, Lou always conducted research before each drug investigation and educated his undercover officers and investigators. He always felt that there was an enormous need for a handy reference manual that described drugs, the way they were manufactured, how they were packaged in the street and what potential street prices would be encountered among other bits of useful information. Because of this need, he created the *Pocketguide to Street Drugs* with all this valuable information and much more. He knows how difficult, time consuming, and almost impossible research can be before and during an investigation so he's done it all in one pocketsized book.

Knowledge is Power, Information is our tool!

Drugs, Crime and the U.S.

The United States, according to the Drug Enforcement Administration, is the world's number one consumer of illicit drugs with a 50% share or higher of the world's market. That, in itself, paint's a sad picture of the drug problem in this country, especially when the U.S. represents only 5% of the world's population. More sadly, is how drug education is part of our basic education curriculum and specialized programs like DARE (Drug Awareness and Recognition Education) and GREAT (Gang Resistance Education And Training) are provided in most schools.

According to drug surveys, 35.6 % of the population over the age of eleven have used illegal drugs. The National Institute on Drug Abuse (NIDA) estimates that about five million Americans suffer from drug addiction. And if the preceding statistics don't paint a frightening picture about drugs effects on society, it is estimated that the war on drugs costs the United States approximately $18 Billion per year while the world's black market illegal drug economy is estimated at $400 Billion per year making up approximately 8% of the global economy.

Criminal Justice experts say that drugs are connected, in some way, to the majority of crimes committed in most communities. Even the world's number one crime, Identity Theft, has emerged as a funding mechanism for drug abusers, drug traffickers and street dealers. It is extensively documented that terrorist organizations use profits from drug manufacture and trafficking to fund operations while drug cartels are heavily involved in other illegal activities such as murder, kidnapping, terrorism, theft, extortion and a host of other crimes.

Controlled Substances Act

In order to understand the regulation and illegal status of the drugs listed in this book, along with the chemicals mentioned that are significant to the manufacture of these drugs, the primary regulatory entity, the Controlled Substances Act is detailed herein.

The Controlled Substances Act (CSA) regulates five classes of drugs. These classes are: narcotics, depressants, stimulants, hallucinogens, and anabolic steroids. Each class has distinguishing properties although the drugs within each class often produce similar effects. The following is the classification listing, and explanation of the classification, of those drugs detailed in this book and other drugs and substances as prescribed by the CSA. There are five schedules of controlled substances. These schedules are identified as Schedule I, II, III, IV, V and are explained below.

Schedule I

Drugs and other substances listed in this schedule have a high potential for abuse, no currently accepted medical use in treatment in the United States, or there is a lack of accepted safety for use of the drug or other substance under medical supervision.

Schedule II

Drugs and other substances listed in this schedule have a high potential for abuse, have a currently accepted medical use in treatment in the United States, a currently accepted medical use with severe restrictions, or abuse of the drug or other substances may lead to severe psychological or physical dependence. Unless specifically excepted or unless listed in another schedule, any of the following substances whether produced directly or indirectly by extraction from substances of vegetable origin, or independently by means of chemical synthesis, or by a combination of extraction and chemical synthesis, are regulated in this schedule.

Schedule III

Drugs and other substances listed in this schedule have a potential for abuse less than the drugs or other substances in schedules I and II., or have a currently accepted medical use in treatment in the United States, or abuse of the drug or other substance may lead to moderate or low physical dependence or high psychological dependence.

Schedule IV

Drugs and other substances listed in this schedule have a low potential for abuse relative to the drugs or other substances in schedule III, or have a currently accepted medical use in treatment in the United States, or Abuse of the drug or other substance may lead to limited physical dependence or psychological dependence relative to the drugs or other substances in schedule III.

Schedule V

Drugs and other substances listed in this schedule have a low potential for abuse relative to the drugs or other substances in schedule IV, the drug or other substance has a currently accepted medical use in treatment in the United States, abuse of the drug or other substance may lead to limited physical dependence or psychological dependence relative to the drugs or other substances in schedule IV.

Along with these drugs, the CSA, which is the principal federal law directed at combating the illicit manufacture and distribution of controlled drugs in the United States, includes chemicals used in the clandestine production of drugs but the controls placed on chemicals are substantially less than those imposed on the previously listed controlled drugs because most of the chemicals have legitimate industrial applications. List I and List II of the Controlled Substances Act contain 35 chemicals.

List I and List II are explained as follows:

List I

The term "'list I chemical'" means a chemical specified by regulation of the Attorney General as a chemical that is used in manufacturing a controlled substance and is important to the manufacture of the controlled substances. Examples of List I Chemicals are: Anthranilic acid, Benzyl cyanide, Ephedrine, Ergonovine, Ergotamine, N-Acetylanthranilic acid, Norpseudoephedrine, Phenylacetic acid, Phenylpropanolamine, Piperidine, Pseudoephedrine, 3,4-Methylenedioxyphenyl-2-propanone, Methylamine, Ethylamine, Propionic anhydride, Insosafrole, Safrole, Piperonal, N-Methylepherdrine, N-methylpseudoephedrine, Hydriodic' Benzaldehyde, Nitroethane, and any salt, optical isomer, or salt of an optical isomer of the chemicals listed above.

List II

The term "'list II chemical'" means a chemical (other than a list I chemical) specified by regulation of the Attorney General as a chemical that is used in manufacturing a controlled substance in violation of this subchapter. Examples of List II Chemicals are: Acetic anhydride, Acetone, Benzyl chloride, Ethyl ether, Potassium permanganate, 2-Butanone, and Toluene.

How to Use this Pocketguide

The *Pocketguide to Street Drugs* was written by a law enforcement officer for law enforcement officers. It is meant to be a reference guide to be used before, during, or after drug investigations, undercover operations, or street drug interdiction and arrests. The most frequently abused drugs that are sold on the streets are referenced in this pocketguide. The drugs detailed are Street Drugs, Club Drugs Predatory Drugs (date-rape drugs), Inhalants, Prescription Drugs, Anabolic Steroids, Over the Counter Drugs and other drugs.

The information on each drug will include the following valuable street information: Photographs, Manufacture, On the Street, Technical name, Appearance, Classification, Controlled Substances Act Schedule, Street names, Legal Uses, Obvious Signs of this Drug Use, Symptoms of Abuse, Risks of Abuse, Addiction, Packaging, Paraphernalia, Cutting Agents, Ingestion Methods, Sought after Effects/High, and Prices per Weight.

Wholesale, retail, and street prices, when listed, are based on the national average according to drug intelligence sources, such as the National Drug Intelligence Center, Drug Enforcement Administration, local police agencies across the United States and Canada, professional experience of the author, and the Office of National Drug Control Policy.

When calculating drug prices, based on the information in this book or current investigations, every law enforcement officer should understand that the further from the source supply, the greater the price of the drug. For example, a small plastic bag (called a slab) of crack cocaine in New York City will be sold by street gang members, such as the Bloods, for as low as $3 to $5 per bag but as high as $20 per bag in northwestern Pennsylvania and Delaware.

Street Drugs

Street Drugs are those drugs that are typically sold in the streets throughout the United States. These drugs are Cocaine, Crack, Heroin, Marijuana, Methamphetamine, and PCP. They make up the largest portion of illicit drugs sold and are connected to the majority of the drug-related violence and crime that has occurred on the streets of the U.S.

Cocaine and Crack, which have long been popular, still remain significant drugs of choice for drug abusers. Since Cocaine is manufactured and imported into the U.S. by dangerous drug cartels, it has a strong nexus to crime, violence, gangs, and murder. Heroin, which has a long history of abuse in the U.S., had greatly diminished as a drug of choice during the 1990s but has made an upsurge in inner cities and other regions in the recent past. The upsurge of heroin is partially due to the higher purity levels and cheaper prices since the South Americans have become major suppliers.

PCP, another long-time abused drug, though not as popular as the others, has made a significant resurgence. The resurgence is mostly due to the proliferation of street gangs and their ability to offer it at inexpensive prices to their drug customers. Marijuana is a steady drug of choice for so many drug abusers and will always remain extremely popular.

Finally, the drug that has been sweeping the U.S., especially throughout middle America, is Methamphetamine. Because it is easy to manufacture and relatively cheap, methamphetamine is sold and abused at alarming and epidemic levels. Methamphetamine, and the other street drugs, will be illustrated in this section, starting with cocaine.

Cocaine

Cocaine in a small personal use Ziploc® bag (top), a razor blade (for cutting lines), a straw (for snorting) and a mirror with lines of cocaine ready to snort.

Cocaine is a stimulant made from the leaves of a Coca plant. The Coca plant is indigenous to the Andean Highland region of South America. The Coca leaves, which are stripped from the Coca bushes, are dried out. The dried leaves are pulverized, often by a mechanical 'weed whacker' or 'trimmer', like those commonly used by landscapers. After the leaves have been pulverized, an alkali (cement or lime is often used) is added and mixed with the leaves so the cocaine alkaloids can be extracted. The resulting cocaine product is then combined with other ingredients such as gasoline, kerosene, sulfuric acid, or potassium permanganate to yield a cocaine 'base'. The cocaine base, which becomes hard and chunky is pulverized and then dissolved in acetone. Hydrolchloric Acid is added and the cocaine is filtered to yield cocaine hydrochloride. The cocaine is generally 75% to 85% pure and can be scraped into a powder when dry. The Cocaine Hydrochloride is usually a beige or off-white crystalline powder dried into solid, compressed, one kilogram bricks (weighing 2.2 lbs) and packaged in plastic and often several layers of duct tape, or other material. In this form it will be shipped out of the region and eventually to the drug consuming markets such as the United States.

On the Street

Solid pieces that are close to 85% pure, whether seized or purchased by an undercover officer, often indicate that the cocaine was yielded from a kilogram. This may indicate that the dealer is close to a larger supply. Generally, flaky texture is indicative of a purer product. Street-level cocaine powder is usually 'cut' or 'stepped on' (diluted) with lactose-type substances such as inositol, mannitol, and lidocaine, in order to expand the product into larger, less potent amounts, and create more profits. The street-level cocaine can range from 30% to 60% pure, depending on how many times it is stepped on and how much 'cut' it is mixed with.

- **Technical name:** Cocaine Hydrochloride
- **Appearance:** White, off-white, light beige flaky powdery substance and powdery and crystalline when diluted with lactose precursors. An faint alkaline scent may be evident.
- **Classification:** Stimulant
- **Controlled Substances Act Schedule:** Schedule II
- **Street names:** Coke, Snow, Powder, Blow, Nose Candy, Girl, Flake, Pariba, Uptown
- **Legal Uses:** Few medicinal applications for eye, nose, and ear surgery but and rarely used today since replaced by safer drugs.

- **Obvious Signs of Cocaine Use:** Dilated pupils, rapid breathing, flushed skin, runny nose, itchy nose
- **Symptoms of Abuse:** Shortness of breath, coughing, chest pains, depression, bleeding, ulcerated mucous membrane, nose bleeds, skin crawling feeling,
- **Risks of Abuse:** Cocaine affects the Central Nervous System (CNS) within 3 to 5 minutes of ingestion by snorting and a euphoric affect is achieved. If injected intravenously, this will happen within 30 seconds. After the 'high' is gone, users can feel irritable, restless, anxious, and nervous. Cocaine causes the blood vessels to constrict, an increased body temperature and heart rate, and increased blood pressure. Cocaine use has also resulted in heart attack, stroke, respiratory failure, and seizures. Using cocaine and alcohol together, often to increase the euphoric affect but the risks of sudden death are increased.
- **Risks of Addiction:** Addictive to Highly Addictive
- **Packaging:** Kilograms are generally packaged in plastic wrap, clear plastic Ziploc® bags, or duct tape. Smaller quantities are contained in plastic Ziploc® bags, tin foils, pyramid papers, dollar bills
- **Paraphernalia:** Clear plastic bags, pyramid papers, tin foil, plastic straws, tiny spoons, razor blades, glass vials, empty ballpoint pen, syringe
- **Cutting Agents:** Lactose, Inositol, Mannitol, Lidocaine, Lactose, Benzocaine

- **Ingestion Methods:** snorted; skin-popped; dissolved in water and injected with a needle; rubbed on gums
- **Sought after Effects/High:** Extreme euphoric effects, total body high, feelings of extreme pleasure, power, excitement, and strength.
- **Street Prices:** *(based on the national average)*

1/10th Gram (Nickel bag):	$5-$10
1/5th Gram (Dime bag):	$10-$40
½ Gram (Quarter):	$25-$40
1 Gram:	$50-$175
1/8 Ounce (8 ball):	$120 to $300
1 Ounce:	$500 to $1000
1/8 Kilo:	$5000
Kilogram:	$15,000 to $35,000

Crack Cocaine

One gram of "rock" (Crack) cocaine

Crack cocaine in a plastic vial (left), rock of crack (center,) a rock in a very small plastic Ziploc® bag (right), crack pipe (top)

Crack-Cocaine, also called rock cocaine, is most commonly made by combining Cocaine Hydrochloride (the street form of cocaine imported into the U.S.) with sodium bicarbonate (Baking Soda). Some drug dealers will add equal parts of their purchased cocaine powder and baking soda with water and mix them together. The mixture is 'cooked' (boiled) on top of a stove in a metal pan, and occasionally placed in a microwave. The cooking evaporates the water and a solid substance called 'crack' is formed after the substance cools down. The reference to crack comes from the fact that when crack-cocaine is smoked it makes a crackling sound. The substance is usually light beige in color and 'rock-like' in texture. While the combining of the two substances (cocaine and baking soda) will yield more of this rocky substance (crack cocaine) it will be half the potency. If the ounce of cocaine powder is 80% pure before it is mixed and cooked with the baking soda then the resulting crack cocaine (Cocaine Hydrochloride and Baking Soda) will have a purity of 40%.

Some street dealers often use the same pot over and over again to cook their supply of crack and many of these pots are damaged, not cleaned, and often scratched. These dealers will scrape the residue left over in the pot and sell it to drug customers who don't have the full price for their personal daily supply of crack. This residue is called 'bazurca' meaning garbage in Spanish and often called 'bazooka' on the street. Some 'bazooka' is even wrapped in empty Bazooka bubble gum wrappers to distinguish its identity from the better crack.

On the Street

Crack cocaine, also called "rock cocaine," is most frequently sold on the street in smaller pieces to frequent users. These users will purchase small, "personal use" amounts from crack dealers. Crack is most frequently smoked. This smoking of crack cocaine with the use of a glass crack pipe, referred to on the street as a 'stem,' will deliver large quantities of the drug directly to the lungs, causing an immediate intense euphoric effect to the user.

- **Technical name:** Cocaine Hydrochloride
- **Controlled Substances Act Schedule:** Schedule II
- **Classification:** Stimulant
- **Appearance:** White, off-white, or light beige rock-like substance that may have a faint scent of alkalide (acid-like) or an aroma of the cutting agent that has been used.
- **Street names:** 1-2-3, 24-7, Badrock, Chips, Cookies, Crack, Crumbs, Crunch-n-Munch, Dice, Gravel, Rock, Tornado
- **Legal Uses:** None
- **Obvious Signs of Crack Use:** Dilated pupils, rapid breathing, flushed skin, runny nose, itchy nose, paranoia

- **Symptoms of Abuse:** Shortness of breath, coughing, chest pains, depression, bleeding, ulcerated mucous membrane, nose bleeds, skin crawling feeling, respiratory failure, lung congestion, wheezing
- **Risks of Abuse:** Inhaling crack cocaine, as with cocaine, affects the Central Nervous System (CNS) but the inhalation will enter the lungs and the euphoric feeling along with the affect on the CNS will be immediate. The "high" is usually gone within a few minutes to fifteen minutes and the smoker can feel irritable, restless, anxious, nervous, and often paranoid. Blood vessels constrict, body temperature increases, heart rate increases, and there is an increased blood pressure. It can result in heart attack, stroke, respiratory failure, and seizures.
- **Risks of Addiction:** Highly addictive
- **Packaging:** Crack is most commonly packaged in small clear plastic Ziploc® bags, plastic baggies, or clear plastic or glass vials usually used to contain small samples of perfume.
- **Paraphernalia:** Clear glass pipe, small round metal screens, matches, lighters, butane torch, 'freebase pipes, clear plastic bags, clear plastic small Ziploc® bags, clear plastic bags, glass vials, plastic vials, tin foil, razor blades
- **Cutting Agents:** Sodium bicarbonate (Baking Soda) is the most common, but some crack manufacturers have used Ammonia or Ether.

- **Ingestion Methods:** Most users place a small piece of the crack in a crack pipe (glass tube) and heat up (vaporize) the crack while inhaling the smoke. Others may place the crack piece in a cigar or cigarette and smoke it.
- **Sought after Effects/High:** Extreme euphoric experience.
- **Street Prices:** *(based on the national average)*

0.065 (Nickel/Slab):	$3-$5 per rock
1/10th Gram (Dime):	$10-$20
1/5th Gram:	$20-$40
½ Gram (Quarter):	$25-$40
1 Gram:	$25-$125
1/8 Ounce (8 ball):	$125 to $200
1 Ounce:	$600 to $1600
1/8 Kilo:	$5500
Kilogram:	$15,000 to $32,000

Heroin

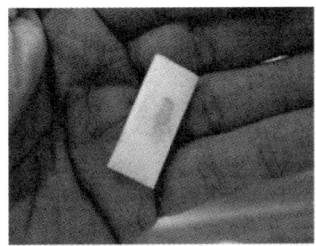

One Dime bag/ glassine envelope with a trademark stamp containing a single hit ($10) of heroin

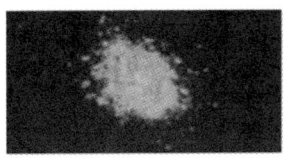

One-hit of heroin powder from a Dime ($10) bag

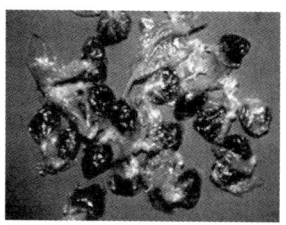

Black Tar heroin packaged for street sale

Heroin has shown a steady increase in popularity in the past 15 years, especially among occasional users. It is estimated that the annual heroin market is as high as 18 million dollars in the U.S. alone. Heroin purity has increased by nearly 35% to place the average purity level at over 30% and a drastic (60%) decrease in price over prices from the 1990s.

Heroin is produced by extracting morphine from the species of the Poppy plant called Papaver Somniferum. This species of poppy, after fertilization drops its flowers and a seed pod is revealed. The seed pod is sliced across the middle to allow milky opium to bleed from the opening. The white milky opium turns brown as it dries. The dried brown opium is scraped and collected on the following day. The dried opium is sold to a processing lab nearby. Here, morphine is extracted from the opium and pressed into small bricks. The bricks are converted to heroin. The heroin is shipped into foreign markets including the U.S.

Heroin is produced in South America (Colombia), Southeast Asia (Burma, Laos, Thailand) Southwest Asia (Pakistan, Afghanistan, Iran) and Mexico. The majority of heroin in the U.S. comes from South America but since "Operation Enduring Freedom," Southwest Asian heroin has increased.

On the Street

Heroin is sold by street dealers with connections to domestic South American, Southeast Asian, Southwest Asian or Mexican suppliers. Many of these suppliers sell at street level drug spots in small quantities up to one ounce quantities. Street level heroin is sold to buyers in glassine envelopes.

- **Technical name:** Diacetylmorphine
- **Controlled Substances Act Schedule:** Schedule I
- **Classification:** Depressant
- **Appearance:** China White appears as a white powder. Black Tar appears as black or dark brown tar-like substance. South American heroin appears as white or beige substance
- **Street names:** H, Big H, Boy, dope, hard stuff, brown sugar, Caballo, China White, schmeck, smack, stuff. Black Tar is called tar, ball, black h, chapapote, chiva, chocolate, goma, mud, tootsie roll

- **Legal Uses:** There are no legal uses for heroin in the U.S.
- **Obvious Signs of Heroin Use:** Slurred speech, drowsiness, white film on mouth, itchy nose, constricted pupils, sweating, flushed face.
- **Symptoms of Abuse:** Track marks, thin, pale skin, collapsed veins, nausea, "nodding," vomiting, malnutrition, sores, infections, diarrhea
- **Risks of Abuse:** HIV/Aids, Hepatitis C, risk of injury from diminished capacity and ability to walk or be alert. Blood infections, hyperventilation, hypothermia, muscle spasms, high blood pressure, stroke, heart attack, death
- **Risks of Addiction:** Highly addictive
- **Packaging:** Large quantities, of heroin, such as kilograms, are packaged in plastic wrap or duct tape. Small quantities are usually packaged in small Ziploc bags, tin foils, or small glassine (waxed) envelopes that are sometimes heat sealed in small clear plastic bags. Tin foil is sometimes used as a container for small street level amounts.
- **Paraphernalia:** Paraphernalia associated with heroin, depends upon the type of user. Some users snort heroin and will possess razor blades and straws like those used with cocaine while intravenous users will possess hypodermic syringes, metal spoons, bottle caps, lighters, butane torches, cotton balls, or cigarette filters. Street level dealers will possess ink pads and rubber stamps to brand their specific product.

- **Cutting Agents:** Procaine, Lidocaine, Mannitol, Caffeine, Lactose, Acetaminophen, Cocaine, Methamphetamine
- **Ingestion Methods:** Heroin can be snorted, swallowed, or injected intravenously as well as skin-popped and free based (chasing the dragon)
- **Sought after Effects/High:** Euphoria, extreme relaxation, ultimate "feel good" feeling
- **Street Prices:** *(based on the national average)*
    .87 grains (1 Dime) in a
        glassine envelope: $10-$20

Mexican Black Tar Heroin: Purity: 20-25%
  Wholesale: Kilo $20,000
  Mexican Ounce ("pedazo" aka *a piece*)
                    $300 to $500
  Retail: Gram $90 to $100
  1/10th Gram $10

Brown Heroin: Wholesale: Kilo $25,000
    Purity average is 30%

China White (Southeast Asian Heroin):
Wholesale: 700-750 Gram Unit $70,000 to $80,000
            300-350 Gram Unit $35,000 to $40,000

Colombian Heroin: 94%
  Wholesale: Kilo - $86,000 to $100,000

Southwest Asian Opium:
  Wholesale: Kilo - $30,000
  Wholesale: 18 Gram Stick - $650 to $800

Marijuana

Dime ($10) Bags of Marijuana ready for sale

Marijuana, by far, is the most frequently used dug in the U.S. It is estimated that Americans spend over $10 Billion a year on marijuana. Marijuana is the term given to the cannabis plant that has a high THC (tetrahydrocannabinol) content that is used as a drug. Cannabis is the botanical genus of the plant with a THC content of less than 1%. It is cultivated for its fiber and oil.

First used for its fiber and seed, cannabis was cultivated in India and Asia over 6,000 years ago. Later it was used as an anesthetic and treatment for several health conditions. During the mid 1800's, cannabis was accepted into western medicine and several pharmaceutical companies developed numerous substances containing marijuana for many illnesses. In 1937, The Marijuana Tax Act was enacted because of the concern over the abuse of marijuana. Later the marijuana substances were dropped from marketing by the pharmaceutical companies In the 1960s, marijuana became widely abused in the U.S. as a psychoactive drug. By the late 1970s, over half of Americans had used marijuana and that widespread abuse continues today, especially among high school age and young adults.

The main source of marijuana in the U.S., today, is grown within the 50 states and the remainder of the supply is imported from Mexico and Canada. There is still some marijuana that is sold in the U.S. that is grown in Colombia, Jamaica, Thailand, Laos, Cambodia and the Philippines. Growing marijuana in the U.S. ranges from the personal use grower to marijuana entrepreneurs who grow up to several thousand plants. There are indoor grows, grows amidst farmland, grows in gardens, yards and even on rooftops. Marijuana grows have even been found on land that is public and privately owned.

To grow marijuana, it is necessary to have the proper location that will facilitate concealment from view of others as well as offering security from law enforcement and thieves. For marijuana growers this could range from a basement hydroponic grow to a plot of land in a hugh forest region. Climate is another consideration for the marijuana grower since a warm climate is necessary. Marijuana plants need at least eight hours of sunlight or proper light provided by artificial lighting. Marijuana grow requires the right types of seeds and the majority of seed suppliers are located in

Canada, Holland, and the United Kingdom. Suppliers from these regions, typically ship their seeds into the U.S. Soil or the proper substitute, a hydroponic setting, is necessary to grow the plants, and of course, water with the right nutrients.

After the plants grow to maturity, they are harvested for their buds and dried in a cool dark environment for approximately seven days. Once the plants are dry, they are ready for packing and sale to dealers.

Hash – Most of the world's hash supply is produced in Southwest Asia. It has been used as a funding mechanism for terrorist organizations in that region for decades. Hash is a result of drying the resin from a marijuana plant and pressing the resin glands together into a small brick or other shape. The THC content of hash is typically 6% in the U.S. but growers boast of a hash supply with a content of 50% - 75%.

A brick of hash

Hash Oil – Hash oil is manufactured by soaking the marijuana in a container of a solvent (acetone, alcohol) and allowing it to soak for several hours. Afterward, the marijuana is removed and the solvent evaporates leaving thick deposits of hash oil that have a consistency that is similar to syrup. Hash oil has a very high level of THC and averages approximately 15% but has been as high as 60%. Hash oil is predominately manufactured in Southwest Asia and Jamaica. A drop or two of hash oil into a cigarette is equivalent to the psychoactive effects of one marijuana joint.

Hash oil above is going to be drained from the solvent

Sinsemilla – Sinsemilla (Spanish, meaning 'without seed') marijuana is harvested from unfertilized female plants. These female plants typically have a high content of THC. An example of such a high content of THC was discovered when the Oregon State Police tested a sample of sinsemilla they seized which indicated a 33.12% content. The sinsemilla marijuana is the result of removing all the male plants from the grow area so they could not pollinate the female plants. Most sinsemilla is grown indoors.

Commercial – Marijuana harvested from in a field of male and female plants is called "commercial" grade. This type of marijuana has a large amount of seeds. Commercial marijuana has shown a THC content of up to 5.11% in recent years. Commercial marijuana is the most common type seized in the U.S. by law enforcement.

Commercial-grade Marijuana

BC Bud – Marijuana harvested in Canada, predominantly in the British Columbia region is called BC Bud. It has a high THC content with recorded high potency of 30%. BC Bud is found often, in the U.S., in the border states near Canada. BC Bud is also referred to as "Quebec Gold" and "Canadian Crop."

On the Street

Marijuana is sold on the street through street corner 'open air' drug spots, residential locations, through beeper and cell phone calls, at night clubs, bars, and schools. A wide variety of people sell Marijuana from all sorts of demographics. Most often, street gang members, organized crime, foreign-born criminals, and others who deal in other drugs sell Marijuana. Larger amounts of Marijuana are generally sold by Mexican drug dealers, gang members, Jamaican drug dealers and others. Marijuana is commonly sold in joints and small personal use quantities packaged in small clear plastic Ziploc® bags.

- **Technical name:** Cannabis Sativa
- **Controlled Substances Act Schedule:** Schedule I
- **Classification:** Stimulant
- **Appearance:** Brownish green leaves
- **Street names:** Weed, Reefer, Smoke, Trees, ganja, grass, herb, leaf, bhang, bush, cannabis, charas, BC Bud, Hyrdo, sess, sins, sinsimilla, Afghani, African Black, Panama Gold, Acapulco Gold, Mota, Mary Jane, Jay, Doobie, grifa, Kif, Juanita, Tea, Texas Tea
- **Legal Uses:** Although some states of Alaska, California, Colorado, Hawaii, Maine, Montana, Nevada, Oregon, Rhode Island, Vermont and Washington, as of January 2006, have approved the use of medical marijuana, U.S. federal laws overrule the law of each state

making the mere possession of medical marijuana a federal crime.

- **Obvious Signs of Marijuana Use:** Bloodshot eyes, sleepy look, sluggish, strong odor of marijuana, chills, dry mouth and throat, difficulty with perception of time
- **Symptoms of Abuse:** Accelerated heart rate for 10 to 30 minutes after ingestion, moderate increase in blood pressure in inexperienced users and lower blood pressure in experienced users, slight drop in body temperature, unable to concentrate
- **Risks of Abuse:** Short term memory loss, anxiety, panic attacks, hallucinations, mood swings, impaired perception
- **Addiction:** moderately addictive
- **Packaging:** Marijuana is mostly packaged in clear plastic Ziploc® bags, from small use sizes to ounce or even pound weight. Marijuana cigarettes, called "joints," are usually hand rolled in rolling papers or rolled in a hollowed-out cigar called a "blunt."
- **Paraphernalia:** Typical marijuana paraphernalia includes small clear Ziploc® bags, paper bags, tin foils, marijuana pipes, bongs, rolling papers, cigars, Kif or stash boxes and roach clips
- **Cutting Agents:** Marijuana is usually smoked on its own but has been mixed with alcohol and other drugs such as PCP, cocaine, and Ecstasy.
- **Ingestion Methods:** Smoking marijuana is the ingestion method of choice. Loading marijuana into

rolling papers (joint) and smoking it is the most common method but smoking a blunt (marijuana inside a cigar shell) is popular. Pipe smoking, bong smoking, and vaporizers are sometimes used, as well as baking marijuana into brownies.
- **Sought after Effects/High:** Feeling "good," euphoria, relaxation
- **Street Prices:** *(based on the national average)*

1 Joint:	$5 to $10
Dime bag:	$10 (makes 1 or 2 joints)
¼ Oz (Quarter):	$30-$40
½ Oz:	$75 to $100
1 Oz:	$125 to $200

Methylamphetamine

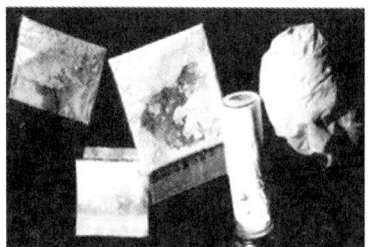

Various forms and colors of powdered meth

A bag of '"Ice," aka "Crystal" Meth. in a small plastic Ziploc® bag

Methylamphetamine, commonly referred to as methamphetamine, is largely produced in clandestine laboratories in Mexico by drug cartels but the remainder is produced in labs across the U.S. The most common precursors for methamphetamine are pseudo ephedrine and ephedrine which are transported into the U.S. and Mexico for production of methamphetamine by illicit laboratories. Some methamphetamine chemists purchase or steal cold medicines to extract the pseudoephedrine or ephedrine from the medicine, but large amounts of these precursors are purchased in Canada, Germany, China, Czechoslovakia and India. Some of the precursors used in production of methamphetamine are still purchased or stolen within the U.S. at legitimate retail stores. These precursors, including pseudo ephedrine, ephedrine, phenyl-2-propanone, methylamine, mercuric chloride, hydrochloric acid, aluminum, isopropanol, sodium hydroxide, anhydrous ammonia, iodine, and red phosphorous are the most common used in the various production methods.

The two main methods used for the production of methamphetamine are briefly described here:

The Hydriotic Acid/Red Phosphorous method uses pseudo ephedrine or ephedrine to create methamphetamine. The pseudo ephedrine, ephedrine or cold medication tablets (containing pseudo/ephedrine) are crushed and the chemical is soaked in a solvent (alcohol, acetone, etc.) and the pseudo ephedrine is extracted and dried into a powder. The powder is mixed with a hydriotic acid (or iodine crystals) and red phosphorous (or hypo phosphorus acid.) The mixture is boiled then filtered. Sodium hydroxide is dissolved in water and added to the solution and a solvent (mineral spirits, etc.) is added to extract, what is now, freebase methamphetamine. The freebase methamphetamine is now added with a hydrogen chloride gas, or similar, to cause the extracted solvent to bubble and white methamphetamine hydrochloride crystals are created. The crystals are filtered and packaged for distribution to dealers.

The Nazi method, also known as The Birch Reduction Method, is a process that uses a pseudo ephedrine solution that was dissolved in anhydrous ammonia. Lithium (or sodium) metal is mixed until the mixture turns blue and then ammonia is allowed to evaporate. The solvent (mineral spirits, etc.) is added to extract the freebase methamphetamine and they mix together causing an oily layer that is poured into a different container. Hydrogen gas is added to bubble the solution until the methamphetamine hydrochloride crystals are formed like the process in the previous method.

The other methods used to manufacture methamphetamine, much less frequently than the two previously described methods are: The P2P Method, the Cold Cook Method, and the Crush and Rush Method.

Typical street level meth lab

There are several variations of methamphetamine on the illicit market. These include:

ICE

Close-up of Crystal meth

Another form of methamphetamine, called Ice or crystal meth, is a purer form of the drug that will have very high purity levels. Ice looks crystalline in appearance and clear in color like small bits of ice or broken glass. Ice is manufactured with an additional process of mixing the powered methamphetamine with a heated solvent to create a more purified solution. When the solution dries, the pure methamphetamine crystals form. Ice, which is chemically identified as dextro methamphetamine HCL is smoked and has a high that lasts as long as eight to sixteen hours.

YABA

Yaba, ("crazy medicine") is a methamphetamine and caffeine tablet created in Southeast Asia for the purpose of giving it to laborers so they could work longer hours in the 1960s. During the 1990s, Yaba became popular in the U.S. Yaba tablets can be swallowed, crushed and snorted, or smoked.

Methamphetamine users, who are frequently getting high, are often called "crank heads." These crank heads often go through a cycle of abuse which varies depending upon the availability of the drug. This cycle includes the initial rush of smoking or injecting the methamphetamine which will last for 5 to 15 minutes, the high that lasts for 4 hours to 15 hours, binging which involves ingesting again, often without sleep, tweaking that manifests itself with paranoia, depression, aggression or even a criminal act (this period can last as long as 24 hours) and finally crashing which results after a few to several days without sleep and ending with a long comatose-like sleep for as long as three days waking up with a strong urge to get high again.

On the Street

Methamphetamine is sold in a variety of communities and can be manufactured from a variety of locations, even in clandestine labs known as 'Mom and Pop' labs. These labs can be found in rural, suburban, or urban residences, barns, garages, trunks of cars, and anywhere that facilitate it. Methamphetamine is sold on the street at street corners, bars, night clubs, out of houses, and often made for personal use.

- **Technical name:** Methylamphetamine Hydrochloride
- **Controlled Substances Act Schedule:** Schedule II
- **Classification:** Stimulant
- **Appearance:** Ice: crystalline, ice-like, clear color that looks like broken glass. Methamphetamine that is most commonly abused is white powder, or a variety of colors depending upon the process and dilutants used
- **Street names:** Meth, crank, ice, crystal chalk, cristy, Hawaiian salt, salt, quartz, speed, ups, diet dust, stay awake, zip
- **Legal Uses:** No legal uses of methamphetamine

- **Obvious Signs of Methamphetamine Use:** Dilated pupils, red eyelids, bloodshot eyes, light sensitive, dry mouth, ultra alert, sweating, teeth grinding, aggressiveness
- **Symptoms of Abuse:** Anxiety, confused, hallucinations, chest pains, delusions, discolored teeth, rapid sign of aging, poor hygiene, sloppy insomnia, mood swings, violent, tremors, skin sores, weight loss
- **Risks of Abuse:** Stroke, seizures, hallucinations, suicide, extreme weight loss, heart attack, deep depression, psychotic behavior, loss of motor control, potential death
- **Addiction:** Highly addictive
- **Packaging:** Methamphetamine is most often packaged in small Ziploc® bags but other forms of packaging has been used such as glassine envelopes, pyramid papers, tin foil or pressed into tablets. Large quantities are packaged in plastic wrap or large Ziploc® bags.
- **Paraphernalia:** Methamphetamine has a multitude of paraphernalia for production and precursors, however, street-level paraphernalia consists of glass pipes for smoking, tin foil free-basing or "chasing the dragon," light bulbs for smoking and spoons and hypodermic syringes for intravenous injection.
- **Cutting Agents:** Generally, methamphetamine is not diluted with other substances after chemical process but some illicit chemists have "cut" methamphetamine with

a variety of substances such as inositol, mannitol, caffeine, or baking soda
- **Ingestion Methods:** Methamphetamine can be smoked, snorted or ingested as well as free based (foiled or chasing the dragon)
- **Sought after Effects/High:** Extreme exhilaration, reduced the need for sleep, weight loss, increase energy, and stay awake for long periods of time
- **Street Prices:** *(based on the national average)*

> ¼ gram sells for $25
> One gram sells for $100
> 8 Ball: (3½ Grams) sells for $300
> One ounce
> (100 plus "hits" of meth) sells for $1700

PCP (Phencyclidine) aka Angel Dust

*A small glass vial (also called a small jar)
of liquid PCP
(called Wet on the street)*

PCP, which is the chemical known as phencyclidine, got its name in San Francisco in 1967 when the intended animal tranquilizer pill was sold on the street at a bay area music festival under the nickname peace pill which became abbreviated to Pea-Cee-P. The pills were believed to be stolen from area hospitals or veterinary offices and diverted to street dealers. By the late 1970s, because of the abuse of the drug, all legitimate manufacturing was terminated.

Today it is manufactured in illicit laboratories, but is still prevalent through street dealers.

PCP is manufactured by combining piperidine, sodium (or potassium) cyanide and distilled water. The solution is chilled on ice and combined with cyclohexanone, sodium metabisulfate and distilled water to create PCC(1-piperidinocyclohexanecarbonnitrile.) The PCC is added to phenylmagnesium bromide in an anhydrous ether solution to yield PCP. PCP is created into powder form, liquid form or pressed into tablets.

On the Street

Street PCP is generally sold in cigarettes or cigars laced in the drug called sherms, packaged as a powder in tin foil or plastic Ziploc® bags or in small glass vials to contain liquid PCP. Cigarettes or marijuana joints soaked in PCP liquid are called "Dip," "Wet," "Wet Sticks," and occasionally "Fry." These, as well as PCP, are commonly sold by street gangs in many urban neighborhoods.

- **Technical name:** Phencyclidine (1-1, phenylcyclohexyl piperidine)
- **Controlled Substances Act Schedule:** Schedule I
- **Classification:** Stimulant
- **Appearance:** PCP can appear as a liquid (light beige to orange) powder or tablets. Some powder is crystalline

in form and light beige, tan or brown in color. PCP has a chemical odor.

- **Street names:** Ace, Angel dust, elephant, embalming fluid, formaldehyde, hog, illy, jet fuel, juice, monkey, ozone, rocket fuel, tac, trank, wack, wet
- **Legal Uses:** No legal uses of PCP
- **Obvious Signs of PCP Use:** Blank stare, excessive eye blinking, sweating, flushed face, drooling, slurred speech, unresponsive and violent.
- **Symptoms of Abuse:** Hallucinations, lack of coordination, confusion, increased heart rate, increased blood pressure, blurred vision, numbness and depression
- **Risks of Abuse:** Coma, anxiety, heart attack, prolonged depression
- **Addiction:** Not physically addictive but psychologically addictive
- **Packaging:** Liquid PCP is packaged in small clear glass vials usually in 2 to 5 ounce sizes. "Wet," "wet sticks" or "dip" is a cigarette or joint that is soaked in PCP. PCP powder is often sealed in tin foils, glassine envelopes or pyramid papers
- **Paraphernalia:** Small glass vials, small Ziploc® bags, dark colored cigarettes
- **Cutting Agents:** Water, distilled water, marijuana, tobacco, acetone, ether and parsley
- **Ingestion Methods:** Liquid PCP is usually smoked. The cigarette or cigar is soaked in the liquid PCP.

Powder PCP can be snorted, smoked, injected or swallowed
- **Sought after Effects/High:** Disassociative mental state, "feel good feeling"
- **Street Prices:** *(based on the national average)*

   1 dose (5mg to 10 mg) sells for $5 to $15 in tablet form
   One gram of powder sells for $20-$30
   One ounce of liquid sells for $200-$300
   One Wet Stick (cigarette) sells for $10-$20 each

Club Drugs

Club Drugs is the name given to a number of drugs that gained popularity in the club scene and rave parties. These drugs, generally, share similar traits that involve an increase of sensory perception of sound, sight, and touch. This increase in sensory perception is believed to enhance the "club" experience. Some of these drugs increase the ability to dance and party for longer durations without getting tired.

The contemporary club scene, rooted in the rave culture, has a variety of its own themes. One such theme goes by the acronym, PLUR, which stands for Peace, Love, Understanding, and Respect. These feelings are supposed to be given to fellow club goers, sometimes, in the form of a physical display brought on by drug-induced feelings. Drugs that are prevalent throughout the club scene are Ecstasy (MDMA), LSD, 2C-B, AMT, 5-MeO, DMT, DPT, AET, and Foxy. Other drugs that are popular in the club scene are described in the Predatory Drugs section. Those drugs are Rohypnol, GHB, and Ketamine.

Ecstasy (MDMA)

*Ecstasy tablets with Adidas logo
embossed on the face*

Ecstasy, also called E or X, is a slang name for the synthetic drug composed of a chemical compound known as MDMA (methylenedioxymethamphetamine). It is a combination of mescaline and amphetamine. It was developed in Germany in the early 1900s as a parent compound for other drugs. During the 1970s, MDMA was prescribed in the U.S. by some psychiatrists as a psychotherapeutic treatment originally intended as a mood enhancer for depression and anxiety patients, and sexual dysfunction patients. At this time, the Food and Drug Administration had not formally approved the use of MDMA in humans.

MDMA production is extremely complex and lengthy. It involves a variety of corrosive chemicals such as acetone, ammonia, calcium chloride, ethanol, hydrochloric acid, magnesium sulfate, methylene chloride, potassium hydroxide, safflower oil, salt, sassafras oil, sodium bicarbonate, sulfuric acid, and other chemicals. It is reported that there is over 20 different processes for manufacturing MDMA. The precursor chemical, which may consist of safrole or piperonal is converted into 3, 4, MDP-2-P and eventually into MDMA.

MDMA is manufactured, most commonly, in tablet form, but can be found in capsule and powder form. The majority of MDMA, approximately eighty percent, sold throughout the world and in the United States, is manufactured in the Netherlands and Belgium with the remainder of MDMA manufactured in Germany, Indonesia, Poland, China, Mexico, Central America, South America, Canada, and right here in the United States.

MDMA, as it is manufactured today by illicit drug laboratories, is often adulterated with a variety of other chemicals. Often, dealers sell 'fake' MDMA tablets which contain some MDMA or no MDMA but may be composed of caffeine, cocaine, codeine, DXM, ephedra, ketamine, MDA, PCP, and other chemicals or harmful adulterants. Approximately ten percent or more of today's supply being sold as MDMA is actually MDA (methylenedioxyamphetamine).

On the Street

MDMA is, by far, the most popular 'Club Drug' and is frequently abused throughout the club and rave scene as well as by many illicit drug users. As previously stated, PLUR (Peace Love Understanding, Respect), associated with the club and rave scene, is also an indication of the use of MDMA. PLUR is often seen on T-shirts, bumper stickers, admission tickets, and other items to indicate that MDMA will be available. MDMA is sold in a variety of shapes, sizes, and colors in the form of a tablet, capsule, or powder. The tablets, which are the majority of the forms encountered, are usually stamped with a logo or icon. The purpose of the logos, icons, and shapes is to attract a young customer and to render the tablet to appear less harmful. MDMA dealers work the high schools, rave parties, and nightclubs, and often use teenaged sales people to develop a customer base. Users of MDMA often take other drugs in conjunction such as Ketamine, PCP, GHB, Cocaine, Nitrous Oxide, Marijuana, and Viagra.

Most MDMA dealers are working for organized crime groups, street gangs, outlaw motorcycle gangs, and individual drug entrepreneurs. The most prolific traffickers are Israeli Mafia members, believed to be headed by Russian Mafia members who immigrated to Israel for the purpose of running large scale MDMA rings. Mexican drug cartels are believed to be involved in MDMA trafficking and have the potential of becoming a major source for MDMA into the U.S.

- **Technical name:** MDMA (methylenedioxymethamphetamine)
- **Appearance:** MDMA comes in a variety of shaped and colored tablets and many with a wide variety of logos stamped on the tablets. The most common logos or icons are: the Mitsubishi Motors logo, The WB (Warner Brothers) logo, a Smiley Face, Flintstones icon, Rolling Stone logo, Superman icon, Motorola logo, Playboy logo, the Money symbol ($) and the M & M logo. The most common shapes are round, shamrock, heart, triangle, pentagon, and a cross. MDMA can also be found in capsule and powder form. Most MDMA tablets are odorless but may have a faint licorice-like odor.
- **Classification:** Hallucinogen and also a Stimulant
- **Controlled Substances Act Schedule:** Schedule I
- **Street names:** Adams, Beans, Disco Biscuit, Doctor, E, Ecstasy, Essence, Go, X, XTC, The Love Pill, The Hug Drug.
- **Legal Uses:** Some psychotherapists prescribe MDMA for patients with anxiety and testing is underway for treatment of cancer patients in order to help them communicate with family members.
- **Obvious Signs of MDMA Use:** Dry mouth, flushed face, sweating, Nystagmus, Dilated pupils, rapid

breathing, teeth grinding, long spells of energy to dance, drinking excessive amounts of water, friendly toward others and strangers.

- **Symptoms of Abuse:** Altered perception of time, decreased sexual activity, increased emotions, blurred vision, high blood pressure, fever, increased heart rate, nausea, restlessness, over-indulgence in liquids, muscle tension.
- **Risks of Abuse:** The release of large quantities of serotonin in the brain while blocking the reuptake of serotonin. Sudden death can result from serotonin toxicity. High fever, Muscle spasms, coma, cardio-vascular collapse, electrolyte imbalance, excessive water in the bloodstream (syndrome of inappropriate antidiuretic hormone secretion) leading to seizures, and heat stroke is common among abusers.
- **Risks of Addiction:** More psychological than physical
- **Packaging:** Plastic bags, blister packs, reusable pill bottles, candy dispensers such a Tic tac boxes and Pez toys as well as bagged candy such as Skittles, Sweet Tarts and M & Ms.
- **Paraphernalia:** Paraphernalia associated with MDMA comes in a wide variety. Tablets can be packaged in plastic bags or secreted in candy wrappers, candy necklaces and bracelets, breath mint or candy dispensers, or lozenge containers. Other paraphernalia include lollipops, candy pacifiers, infant pacifiers, and mouth guards to diminish teeth grinding brought about by

MDMA use. Light sticks, flashlights, glow in the dark jewelry, and blinking lights enhance visual perception. Dust masks with vapor rub spread on the inside are used to enhance the effects of the drug. MDMA users will possess 'Come Down Kits' to reduce the symptoms of MDMA. These kits can contain Viagra to increase the MDMA decreased sex drive, caffeine to cut the MDMA powder, Magnesium and Carnitine to balance serotonin levels, and mood enhancers to decrease the depression resulting from withdrawal.

- **Cutting Agents:** MDMA should not be adulterated with any other chemicals but illicit laboratories often use a variety of substances to manufacture MDMA. It is not uncommon for MDMA tablets to be laced partially, or entirely, with cocaine, codeine, DXM, ephedra, or even be passed off as MDMA when the tablets are actually amphetamine, methamphetamine, or other chemicals.
- **Ingestion Methods:** Tablets and capsules are swallowed orally while powder can be injected or snorted. The psychological effects of MDMA are felt within 30 to 45 minutes after ingestion with the most intense effects occurring within 60 to 90 minutes after ingestion and may persist for two hours wearing down after four to six hours later.
- **Sought after Effects/High:** Euphoria, enhanced sexuality and sensuality, positive feelings, extreme relaxation, suppress inhibitions.

- **Street Prices:** *(national average)*

  Wholesale:

  1 Gram of Crystal MDMA: Avg Purity of 95% is $225
  1 Boat: (1,000 tablets) Avg Purity of 60% is $5000

  Retail:

  1 Tablet: (25mg to 75mg) Avg Purity of 50 to 75% is $5-10
  1 Tablet: (75 mg to 175 mg) Avg Purity of 50 to 75% is $10-50

LSD

Blotter paper with 12 individual "hits" of LSD

LSD, is a powerful hallucinogenic drug that affects the Central Nervous System from multiple sites. It is a semi-synthetic substance that gained popularity in the 1960's. Previously, the Sandoz Company was marketing LSD as a treatment for schizophrenia. The U.S. Military conducted tests of LSD for use in mind control and non-military scientists conducted investigations which proved that LSD was not as effective or safe as advertised. With some respected scientists, actors, musicians and academics praising the use of the drug as a self-exploration experience, popularity grew and abuse became widespread. In 1965, its non-medical use was outlawed and the Sandoz Company withdrew its support of the drug.

The majority of LSD is reportedly manufactured in Northern California but LSD seizures have been recorded across the U.S. Several processes exist to manufacture LSD but the preferred methods are the Curtis Reaction or the Garbrecht Synthesis. These methods require a combination of chemicals and toxic chemicals such as, benzene, chloroform, ether, glacial acetic acid, hydrochloric acid, sodium carbonate, and sodium nitrate. The LSD is later converted into LSD crystals.

On the Street

Wholesale dealers usually purchase their supply of LSD direct from the illicit manufacturer. The dealers purchase multi gram weight of LSD and these dealers sell to gram weight LSD dealers. The gram weight LSD dealers convert the pure crystal LSD into liquid form and place the liquid LSD on blotter paper to create multi-tab (dose) sheets. These sheets are usually one hundred to one thousand doses. One sheet usually consists of 100 perforated squares (each square is a dose) and a count of 1,000 squares is called a book often sold as 10 sheets of 100 squares a piece. LSD has regained popularity because of the rave culture and club scene. Because LSD is degraded by light it is usually "dropped" on blotter paper within a short period of time before sale to insure its potency.

- **Technical name:** d-lysergic acid diethylamide
- **Controlled Substances Act Schedule:** Schedule I
- **Classification:** Hallucinogen
- **Appearance:** Pure LSD crystals are clear or white and odorless. Less pure LSD can be yellow, tan, or even black. Liquid street LSD is sold on blotter paper with small perforated squares of different cartoon characters or icons on each dose.
- **Street names:** Acid, Big D, Blotter, Blue heaven, California sunshine, cube, D, dose, dot, L, microdot, paper acid, royal blue, Sandoz, sheet acid, sid, spots, sunshine, tab, ticket, window pane
- **Legal Uses:** No legal uses of LSD in the U.S.
- **Obvious Signs of LSD Use:** Flushed face, sweating, dilated pupils, apparent sensitivity to sounds and sight

- **Symptoms of Abuse:** Hallucinations, paranoia, high blood pressure, increased pulse rate and respiration. Flashbacks, from a previous LSD experience can occur weeks to years after but for a few seconds, hearing sounds that are not there.
- **Risks of Abuse:** Extreme hallucinations, paranoid, panic attacks, recurring flashbacks, seizures, memory disorders
- **Risks of Addiction:** not generally physically addictive
- **Packaging:** Street (retail) LSD is usually in the form of tabs or hits (one dose), sheets (100 doses) or books (10 sheets of 100 doses) and kept in film canisters because LSD is sensitive light and can be destroyed by heat
- **Paraphernalia:** Blotter paper with perforations that have small half inch squares on it. Each square has a cartoon character, icon, or other picture on it.
- **Cutting Agents:** LSD is not usually diluted by the dealer, but some dealers have been reported to "cut" their LSD liquid with 20% water to increase its retail value.
- **Ingestion Methods:** The most common way that LSD is ingested is by placing a "hit," "tab" or "ticket" on the tongue and the drug is absorbed into the mucous membrane. It can also be added, liquid form, to sugar cubes, liquids and other foods or placing a drop in the eye.
- **Sought after Effects/High:** Psychedelic experience, mind exploration

- **Street Prices:** *(based on the national average)*

    1 dose/hit/tab (20 mcg to 80 mcg sells for $2 to $5
    1 Sheet (10 hits) sell for $10 to $20
    1 Book (100 hits) sells for $100 to $250

2C-B (Nexus)

2C-B embossed to look like Ecstasy

Manufacture

2C-B, commonly called Nexus, was designated a Schedule 1 drug in 1995. During that time, it dropped in popularity, most likely because of the difficulty in procuring the drug. In 1999, according to the DEA, seizures of the drug have increased. 2CB is a popular club drug often sold to unsuspecting illicit drug consumers as MDMA. 2CB is illicitly manufactured in Canada and the United Kingdom. 2CB was created, in the early 1970s, by an American pharmacologist named Alexander Shulkin as a psychedelic drug to assist people in self-knowledge and psychological insight. 2CB is synthesized by combining a solution of 100g of 2,5-dimethoxybenzaldehyde in 220g nitromethane treated with 10g of anhydrous ammonium acetate and heated on a steam bath for two and a half hours with occasional swirling.

On the Street

2CB is sold on the street in capsules, tablets, and powder, and often taken in conjunction with MDMA tablets to enhance the feeling of euphoria, psychedelic effects, and often as a sexual enhancement drug. Many users purchase the drug through internet 'digital dealers'. 2CB is not as prevalent on the street as MDMA for several reasons. It is more difficult to make, it is not as popular as ecstasy, and it is not manufactured extensively as MDMA.

Usually taken in small doses, like 8 to 10 mg, 2CB is a psychoactive drug that produces increased sensations such as auditory, visual, olfactory, and tactile sensations. It can also make that person extremely intoxicated. A very small dose of 4 mg can make the user become passive and relaxed. Doses of 20 to 30 mg cause strong hallucinations and fear.

- **Technical name:** 4-bromo-2, 5 dimethoxyphenethylamine
- **Appearance:** White powder form, capsules, and tablets are the most common on the street. Off white pills with brown specks; pink, red or purple tablets; Small off-white, thick tablets, will have a variety of logos similar to MDMA tablets; Clear, yellow, or blue and gray capsules.
- **Classification:** Hallucinogen
- **Controlled Substances Act Schedule:** Schedule I
- **Street names:** Nexus (most common), 2's, Bees, BDMPEA, Bromo, Cee-Beetje, Cloud 9, Erox, , MTF, Performax, Spectrum, Synergy, Toonies, Utopia, Venus, Zenith
- **Legal Uses:** Some psychologists prescribed 2CB during the 1970s but it has not been legal to prescribe since its became a Schedule I controlled substance.
- **Obvious Signs of 2-CB Use:** Smiling, giggling, laughing, coughing, delusional, irrational, muscle clenching, nasal pain, nausea. Users claim that objects appear to be leaving a visual trail behind them and often an appearance of geometric patterns moving or breathing. Listening to music under the influence of 2-CB causes the user to see normal colors, patterns, and movements as distorted.
- **Symptoms of Abuse:** Slight Pupil dilation, intoxication, slight to extreme hallucinations, anxiety, prolonged irrational behavior, claustrophobia.

- **Risks of Abuse:** High
- **Addiction:** More psychological than physical
- **Packaging:** Plastic bags, blister packs, reusable pill bottles, candy dispensers such a Tic tac boxes and Pez toys as well as bagged candy such as Skittles, Sweet Tarts and M & Ms.
- **Paraphernalia:** Paraphernalia associated with 2-CB is the same as paraphernalia associated with MDMA. Tablets can be packaged in plastic bags or secreted in candy wrappers, candy necklaces and bracelets, breath mint or candy dispensers, or lozenge containers. Other paraphernalia include lollipops, candy pacifiers, infant pacifiers, and mouth guards to diminish teeth grinding brought about by its. Light sticks, flashlights, glow in the dark jewelry, and blinking lights enhance visual perception. Dust masks with vapor rub spread on the inside are used to enhance the effects of the drug.
- **Cutting Agents:** The only cutting agents are those used in the manufacture of the drug.
- **Ingestion Methods:** Powder is snorted. Sometimes the powder from the capsules are removed and snorted while most capsules and tablets are swallowed.
- **Sought after Effects/High:** Users report a feeling of being "in touch" with themselves and their emotions and erotic sensations and feelings of being "in one's body." With higher doses (15-30mg), 2C-B produces intense visual effects. Moving objects leave "trails" behind them. Surfaces may appear covered with geo-

metric patterns, and may appear to be moving or "breathing." Colors may appear from nowhere. Users often say they can "see" the music.

- **Prices per Weight:** *(based on the national average)*

Retail

    1 10 mg tablet or capsule is sold for $10 -$30
    1 Gram can cost $100-$500

Wholesale
    1 Gram can cost $75 to $300

Other increasingly popular "club" drugs belong to the chemical classification known as tryptamines. Most tryptamines are derived from plants (mushrooms) and seeds but some can be synthetically produced. These substances are psychoactive and can cause hallucinations.

Tryptamines are sold in a variety of drugs, especially at night clubs, bars, raves, college campuses, and schools. Tryptamines come in tablet form (similar to ecstasy), and powder form. They are classified as Schedule I hallucinogens. The following are those tryptamines that are prevalent throughout the club scene.

AMT (Alpha-Methyltryptamine) is also known as Spirals, Alpha, Alphameth, and AMT. It is a psychoactive drug.

AMT is usually sold in odorless white powder form. It is ingested orally or smoked in a pipe or bong. AMT is abused for its ability to increase energy and creates stimulation. A person under the influence of AMT will have dilated pupils, blurred vision, and may be yawning. AMT can cause anxiety, nausea, vomiting, muscle aches, headaches, and jaw clenching. A user can become psychologically addicted. It is often packaged in tin foils, glassine envelopes, small paper envelopes (Pyramid papers), or small plastic bags. It can aslo be placed in capsules and swallowed. Paraphernalia associated with AMT consists of glasss pipes, bongs, glass vials, and capsules.

- **Street Prices:** *(based on the national average)*

    1 dose of AMT (2 mg) is $5 to $20
    1 gram of AMT is $100 to $750

5-MeO-AMT (5-methoxy-alpha- methyltryptamine) is also known as 5-MeO, Alpha, alpha-O, or O-DMS. 5-MeO, has an alternate chemical name of alpha, 0-dimethylserotonin. It is a psychoactive drug. It is sold in an odorless white powder in small glass (or plastic) vials. It can be dissolved in water or alcohol and soaked into sugar cubes, candy, or blotter paper (like LSD). It can be ingested orally, snorted, or smoked. Tablets are also sold occasionally and can be crushed if the user so desires. A person under the influence of 5MeO will have obvious signs of hearing and seeing difficulty because of the drug's ability to cause an enhanced visual and auditory perception and psychological alteration. It is a psychologically addictive drug that causes a user's sexual inhibitions to diminish. 5MeO can cause nausea, diarrhea, vomiting, and hallucinations. 5MeO is often sold to unsuspecting buyers as Ecstasy. These tablets are often sold in candy wrappers, in lozenge containers, or sold in sugar cubes or candy capable of being soaked with the liquid form. Paraphernalia used is candy, sugar cubes, blotter paper, glass pipes and bongs (for smoking) and glass (or plastic) vials usually capable of containing at least a quarter ounce or more.

- **Street Prices:** *(based on the national average)*

  1 dose is 2 mg to 4.5mg and sells for $10 to $25.

Foxy (5-methoxy-N, N-diisopropyltryptamine) is the common street name for this Schedule I hallucinogenic drug. Foxy is usually sold in powder form, tablets, or in capsules. The powdered form is usually mixed with other colored powders resulting in a variety of tablet and capsule colors. The tablets are embossed with a variety of icons and logos similar to ecstasy tablets. The most common logo seen has been a spider or alien head. Foxy is ingested orally but may be smoked or snorted. The effects of Foxy begin within 20 to 30 minutes of ingestion and last for 3 to 6 hours. The typical abuser is a teenager or young adult involved in the club or rave scene seeking a milder LSD-type effect unless the dose is increased to 12 mg or higher. Obvious signs of a Foxy user are dilated pupils, talkativeness, visual problems, hearing problems, and distorted sight. The effects and symptoms are hallucinations, vomiting, diarrhea, emotional distress, lack of sexual inhibitions and anxiety. Foxy is often called Foxy methoxy, Methoxy, Spider, and Alien. It is sold as to unsuspecting users as ecstasy but mostly as its own distinct drug.

- **Street Prices:** *(based on the national average)*

    1 dose is 6 mg and sells for $5 to $10.

DMT, DET, DPT, and AET are the other tryptamines sold throughout the club scene and at rave parties but with much less frequency. They have similar effects to the other tryptamines but their effects do not last as long. DMT (dimethyltryptamine), because of its milder effects, is called the "businessman's high" or "businessman's trip." DET (diethyltryptamine) is an analog of DMT with milder but similar effects that lasts, also, for about an hour. DPT (N, N-dipropyltryptamine) has similar effects as DMT, DET, and AET, but is infrequently sold since it has been reported to leave the user with an ammonia-like body odor. AET (alpha-ethyltryptamine) is the least sold tryptamine. These tryptamines, generally, sell for $5 to $15.

Sold on the street as alternatives to ecstasy, and to create more markets for drug dealers, several other hallucinogenic drugs have been surfacing, in recent years, on the club drug scene. These drugs are DOB, BZP, 2C-T-7.

DOB (2, 5-dimethoxy-4-bromoamphetamine) is a phenethylamine that was synthesized in 1953. It is commonly known as STP (Serenity, Tranquility, and Peace). It is so named because it relieves depression and can cause the user to think clearer and increase attention span. DOB is sold in a variety of forms. In powder form, DOB is sold in small Ziploc® bags, tin foils, paper envelopes, and small glass (or plastic) vials. The powder can be snorted, swallowed, and even injected when it is dissolved in water. It is sold, most commonly in liquid form and dropped on blotter paper (like LSD) and ingested on the tongue. DOB has also been sold in tablets and suppositories. When taking DOB in a suppository (rectally) form, it takes effect quicker and lasts longer. DOB is also known as Bromo, Dob, but most commonly, STP. DOB is addictive and can cause a host of symptoms and health risks. It can cause increased energy, mental clarity, mild hallucinations, euphoria, and feelings of affection but lead to anxiety, memory loss, nausea, headaches, muscle tension, teeth grinding, irrational behavior, Glaucoma, and stroke.

- **Street Prices:** *(based on the national average)*

    1 dose is .75 mg to 1.75 mg and sells for $10 to $50.

BZP (N-benzylpiperazine) is a synthetic stimulant that is several times more potent than amphetamine. BZP is a Schedule I controlled substance and has a high risk of abuse. BZP is also known as AZ, Frenzy, and Nemesis, and is sold, mostly, as tablets with logos or icons embossed on the face. BZP is often laced with other drugs, such as TFMPP (1-3-, trifluoromethylphenyl piperazine), an hallucinogen or other drugs including cocaine and DXM (dextromethorphan) which is found in cough syrup. BZP is often sold as Ecstasy to unsuspecting users. BZP has also been sold in powder and capsule form. BZP is abused, mostly, by teenagers and young adults, but has been found to be used by other club goers seeking a stronger high than Ecstasy. BZP is taken orally, snorted, or even smoked. It can cause obvious symptoms, such as papillary dilation, flushed face, excess blinking and dizziness and health risks that include insomnia, irregular heartbeats, delusions, hallucinations, and paranoia. High doses of BZP, often 200 mg or more, can cause overdose leading to stroke or death. The effects of BZP can last between 2 to 8 hours.

- **Street Prices:** *(based on the national average)*

1 dose is 20 mg and sells for $5 to $25.

2C-T-7 (2,5-dimethoxy-4-(N) propylthiophenethylamine) is a synthetic drug with hallucinogenic properties. It is a Schedule I drug and is a member of the phenethylamine class of chemical compounds. 2C-T-7 is also known on the street as 2C, Beautiful, Blue Mystic, Lucky 7, PT-DM-PEA, Red Raspberry, Tripstasy, Tweetybird, Tweetybird mescaline, 7th Heaven and 7-Up. It is sold in powder form in small glass vials or small Ziploc® bags. It is also sold in capsules and sometimes tablets with logos or icons. It is mostly sold at raves and clubs but has been frequently sold at high school and college campuses. 2C-T-7 causes the user to experience a variety of hallucinogenic effects such as delusions, sensory impairment, sight and sound enhancement, and out of body feelings. Users appear to be sleepy and tense with a tightened jaw and flushed face. It can also cause nausea, vomiting, irritability, irregular heartbeat, anxiety, depression, insomnia, memory loss, stroke, and death.

- **Street Prices:** *(based on the national average)*

    1 dose is .20 mg and sells for $10 to $25.

Predatory Drugs

The term Predatory Drugs refers to drugs that are frequently used to facilitate the crime of sexual assault against another. Although these drugs are also popular throughout the "club" and "rave" scene, they pose a more serious threat because of their use in drug-assisted sexual assaults. These predatory drugs, which can be identified as **GHB (GBL and BD are also included), Rohypnol, Ketamine, Soma, and Quaaludes**, have been given to an unsuspecting victim to render the victim helpless or extremely weak. These drugs are often administered to a victim by dropping a dose into the victim's drink at a nightclub, party, or bar. Predators often "feed" the victim several drinks to make the victim less alert and more intoxicated to assist in slipping something into the victim's drink. The effects of alcohol, which is also a drug, increase the effectiveness of the predatory drug used. After the drug takes effect on the victim, who may become extremely intoxicated or unconscious, the predator now has the ability to take advantage of the victim. Often, predators have raped, sexually assaulted, or sexually abused their victims and frequently committed acts of robbery and theft from the victim. In many cases, victims may not remember what had happened or may be unclear of the circumstances because of the drug induced intoxication or unconsciousness.

Alarmingly, these drugs are being sold on college campuses, high school campuses, playgrounds, parties, raves, night clubs, and middle schools but can be purchased over the internet. This availability affords predators of all ages the opportunity to commit their acts throughout a host of settings. In 1990, the Food and Drug Administration decided to identify GHB as an illegal drug and called for its removal from store shelves but by the late 1990s it became extremely popular as a 'club drug' through the rave culture.

Also associated with predatory crimes, mostly rape, are common household products purchased at any pharmacy or convenience store. These products, Visine, Equate, or other eye drops or solutions contains **Tetrahydrozoline** or other chemicals like **Naphazoline** and **Oxymetazoline** are dropped in a victim's drink to cause abrupt loss of consciousness. This technique is called "dripping" or "dropping."

GHB

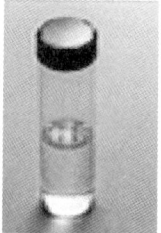

GHB Liquid

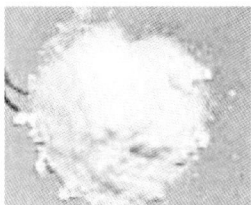
GHB Powder Form

GHB, Gamma-Hydroxybutyrate, is a metabolite which occurs naturally in the human body that was used in the 1960s as an aid in child birth and a treatment for sleep disorders and drug abuse. It gained popularity among body builders as a chemical that stimulated growth hormones. During the 1980s GHB was sold over the counter in health food stores. This is when the abuse of GHB was first encountered. In 1990, the Food and Drug Administration decided to identify GHB as an illegal drug and called for the removal of it from store shelves, however, by the late 1990s it became extremely popular as a 'club drug' through the rave culture.

Gamma Butyrolactone (GBL) and Sodium Hydroxide (NaOH) were originally purchased separately, or in kits, and were sold over the internet or through magazines. Upon mixing these chemicals together, a clear liquid resulted that contained .85 to 1.3 grams of GHB per teaspoon. The most common form of GHB on the street results from the diversion of GBL and NaOH from commonly sold chemicals to yield, what is prevalent on the street. This chemical compound of GHB is 4-hydroxybutyrate acid sodium salt. This compound is added to water and then lemon juice or vinegar is added to neutralize the mixture. GBL itself, and a chemical called BD (1, 4 -butanediol), when ingested orally, is automatically metabolized by the body into GHB.

The processes by which an illicit chemist creates GHB can be found on the internet but the most common application includes GBL as a precursor which can be extracted from a variety of solvents, resins, such as metal cleaning products, paint strippers, and products found in textile manufacture. The FDA issued a recall on all products for human consumption which contained GBL, such as toothpastes, making it more difficult for traffickers to obtain GBL for the manufacture of GHB. Many traffickers turned to BD (1, 4 -butanediol) as a precursor chemical to create GHB. BD, however, is not regulated and can be found in a number of chemical products like solvents, polyurethanes, resins, and other pharmaceuticals. The most common chemical or trade names for BD, found on labels of solvent type products, are dihydroxybutane, butylenes glycol, tetramethylene-glycol, and sucol-B.

On the Street

GHB, in liquid form, is sold on the street in water-type squeeze bottles, lotion bottles, eye droppers, and small glass vials capable of holding 1 to several ounces of liquid GHB. Liquid GHB is the most common form on the street, It also known as a 'Predatory Drug' or date-rape drug because of its use by adding to a drink of an unsuspecting victim which can cause the victim to become sleepy, intoxicated and unconscious. GHB is common among the club scene, rave scene and trance scene. Often, people who attend these scenes, will take part in marathon sessions of club hopping, dancing, and trance-parties (lengthy highs). GHB is often added to a flavored liquid, or drink, to mask the salty taste and avoid detection. GHB substitutes have also been sold under a variety of names such as Revivarant, Renewtrient, Fire Water, Serenity, Thunder Nectar, Verve, Weight Belt Cleaner, Blue Nitro, Fire Water, Enliven, Invigorate, Remforce, and Xyrem (Sodium Oxybate).

- **Technical name:** Gamma-Hydroxybutyrate
- **Controlled Substances Act Schedule:** Schedule I, Schedule III controlled substance when used as a prescribed medication.
- **Classification:** Stimulant
- **Appearance:** A clear liquid that can be odorless and tasteless but may have a slightly salty taste and an odor of lemon juice or vinegar.

NOTE: To test for GHB in a water bottle, shake the bottle strongly, and if the water becomes cloudy, GHB may be present in the water.

- **Street names:** Easy-lay, soap, liquid X, vita-G, get-big, Georgia Home Boy, Get Her Boned, Get Huge Biceps.
- **Legal Uses:** Liquid GHB, marketed under the name, Xyrem (Sodium Oxybate), is a medically formulated chemical used in the treatment of patients with cataplexy (excessive sleep) attacks in patients with narcolepsy.
- **Obvious Signs of GHB Use:** Sweating, Tremors, difficulty breathing, Speech and motor skill interference, agitated, combative, confusion, and weakness.
- **Symptoms of Abuse:** Vomiting
- **Risks of Abuse:** Cardiac and respiratory depression, stroke, and death.
- **Risks of Addiction:** Addictive.
- **Packaging:** Liquid GHB is usually contained in water and sport drink bottles, eye dropper bottles, glass vials, or other squeeze bottles. Powder form can be pressed into a tablet or sealed in tin foils, glassine envelopes or other packaging consistent with holding a powder.
- **Paraphernalia:** Eye droppers, squeeze bottles, clear glass vials, pyramid papers, tin foils, Ziploc® bags and plastic bags.
- **Cutting Agents:** GHB is seldom adulterated with other substances except water of drinks.

- **Ingestion Methods:** Most users mix the liquid GHB into drinks, water bottles, and other liquids while ingestion of the powder form of GHB can be done orally, snorted, or injected intravenously.
- **Sought after Effects/High:** Relaxation effect that is similar to Alcohol intoxication, euphoria, reduced inhibitions, enhanced sensuality and sexuality, and increased sensory stimulation. Use as a growth hormone.
- **Street Prices:** *(based on the national average)*

1 capful (1 teaspoon/5ml)	$2 to 30 per capful
1 Small glass vial (1 oz)	$60
1 Gram of powder:	$75
1 Gallon of Liquid:	$100 to 1000

Ketamine

Powdered Ketamine

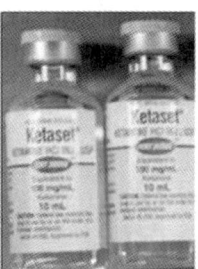

Liquid Ketamine

Ketamine, which is well known under the slang name of Special K, is short for Ketamine Hydrochloride. It is legally used as a veterinary anesthetic and is has a combination of stimulant, depressant, hallucinogenic, and analgesic properties. Its commercial production can be found in Belgium, China, Colombia, Germany, Mexico, and the United States. Ketamine is a popular club drug among constituents of the rave and club scenes. It is also one of the 'Predatory Drugs' used in date rapes. Because of its sedative and disassociative properties, Ketamine easily facilitates a defenseless demeanor on unsuspecting victims often induced through spiking the victim's drink by the predator criminal. Ketamine is difficult to detect in the urine and blood after 48 hours from the original ingestion.

To produce Ketamine Hydrochloride, an illicit chemist would need an extensive laboratory and have a lot of time to conduct the process. This difficult scenario for producing

Ketamine makes illicit laboratories rare in the United States. The most common way, of illicitly acquiring the drug in the U.S., is through thefts such as burglaries and employee theft at veterinarian offices and animal hospitals. Illegal importation of diverted supplies of Ketamine arrive into the U.S. through Mexico. Ketamine has also been sold over the internet.

On the Street

Ketamine is usually sold and passed on through close social settings and personal relationships but drug dealers who mainly work the rave and club scenes will cautiously sell Ketamine to those who want to purchase the drug.

- **Technical name:** Ketamine Hydrochloride
- **Controlled Substances Act Schedule:** Schedule III
- **Classification:** Depressant
- **Appearance:** White Powder or clear liquid form is the most common but some users evaporate the liquid form resulting in crystals.
- **Street names:** Special K, K, Ket, Kit Kat, Lady K, Vitamin K, Purple, Cat valium, Super acid, Super C, Super K, cat tranquilizers, Ketaset, Ketalar
- **Legal Uses:** It is used as a veterinary anesthetic.
- **Obvious Signs of Ketamine Use:** Dilated pupils, dizziness, garbled speech, sweating, loss of time perception, and disorientation.

- **Symptoms of Abuse:** Nausea, dizziness, low breathing rate, loss of motor skills, slurred speech, paranoia, hallucinations.
- **Risks of Abuse:** Flashbacks, Physical tolerance, psychological dependence, convulsions, vomiting, coma, death.
- **Addiction:** Addictive
- **Packaging:** Ketamine is usually found in small glass vials for liquid and powdered form and small Ziploc® bags, plastic baggies, glassine envelopes, paper, dollar bills, and aluminum foils. Ketamine can also be found in capsules. Commercial Ketamine is distributed in injection bottles and small glass vials.
- **Paraphernalia:** Paraphernalia associated with Ketamine is glass vials, bottles, droppers and when in powder form paraphernalia is consistent with other powdered drugs.
- **Cutting Agents:** Ketamine is seldom adulterated with any other substance other than water or a drink.
- **Ingestion Methods:** Ketamine powder is cut into lines, called bumps on the street, and snorted. The effects, by snorting, manifest in 5 to 10 minutes. It can also be smoked when commonly mixed into a cigarette of marijuana joint. Liquid Ketamine can be injected into the muscles or veins which affects the person within 3 minutes and lasts for 45 to 90 minutes. It can be mixed into drinks and the effects are felt within 5 to 20

minutes and last for up to 90 minutes. Sometimes, Ketamine is rectally inserted.
- **Sought after Effects/High:** Mild hallucinations that last for 10 to 30 minutes; Out of body experience.
- **Street Prices:** *(based on the national average)*

One Single Dose (140 mg) costs $3 to $7
10 ml bottle costs $10 to $120
1 Gram can range from $15-$300,
   with an average of $85

Rohypnol

Rohypnol is a trade name for the depressant drug (flunitrazepam). It is referred to as "roofies" on the street. It affects the central nervous system. Rohypnol first became popular among drug abusers in the U.S. during the early 1990s as a "come down" drug for the depression following the withdrawal from cocaine, heroin and methamphetamine. It is believed that rohypnol received its nickname "roofies" because it was smuggled into the U.S. by roofers and construction workers working in South Florida after Hurricane Andrew.

Rohypnol is not a legal drug in the U.S., but it is sold legally in 70 countries including Mexico. Rohypnol is mostly transported across the Mexican border and sold at night clubs, raves and where other "designer" of "club" drugs are sold. It gained national attention as a "date rape" drug because of its documented use in many rapes and sexual assaults across the U.S. The pill is placed (in solid or powder) in the unsuspecting victim's drink and the effects are experienced in 20 to 30 minutes. The effects are at their strength in 2 hours and can last for 8 hours.

On the Street

Rohypnol is abused by people ranging from age 13 to 30 and often used or sold at parties, bars, night clubs, college campuses, high schools and raves.

- **Technical name**: Flunitrazepam
- **Controlled Substances Act Schedule:** Schedule IV
- **Classification:** Depressant
- **Appearance:** A dull green caplet with "542" imprinted on one side. The caplet has a blue core that turns a clear liquid blue when dropped in a drink

- **Street names:** Roofies, roches, ruffles, ropies, R-2, R-1, The forget me pill, circles, lunch money drug, pingas, Reynolds, roaches, roachies, wolfies, Mexican valium
- **Legal Uses:** No legal uses in the U.S. but sold as a treatment for depression in other countries.
- **Obvious Signs of Rohypnol Use:** Drowsiness, excitability, lack of coordination, dizzy
- **Symptoms of Abuse:** Memory loss, nightmares, tremors, dizziness
- **Risks of Abuse:** Susceptibility to assault due to diminished alertness, extreme drowsiness, or sleep, amnesia, low blood pressure
- **Addiction:** Physically and psychologically addictive
- **Packaging:** Pills are often secreted in pill bottles among legal prescriptions to hinder their identification
- **Paraphernalia:** Colored liquids, mortar and pestle pill cutters to crush the pills to make a powder
- **Cutting Agents:** Water and liquids
- **Ingestion Methods:** Caplets are swallowed in whole or crushed into powder and added to a drink to dissolve. Some users dissolve the crushed powder in water and inject the drug intravenously
- **Sought after Effects/High:** Relaxation, sleep, diminish inhibitions, sedative properties
- **Street Prices:** *(based on the national average)*

  1 tablet (1mg) $6-$10

Soma

Soma is a trade name for a drug that is known as Carisoprodol. It is a muscle relaxant and Central Nervous System depressant prescribed by doctors for the relief of discomfort, muscle spasms, and stiffness as a result of injuries. Although Soma is not controlled by the federal government, it is a scheduled drug in several states (GA, FL, HA, ID, IN, KY, MA, MN, NM, OK, OR, WV). It is usually sold in tablet form with SOMA and 37 WALLACE imprinted on opposite sides but is also sold in a liquid. It is manufactured in the U.S. but frequently smuggled into the U.S. through Mexico. Soma can also be purchased over the internet.

Soma can produce sedative effects on a person, and when coupled with alcohol, it is easily capable of facilitating a sexual assault or other crime. Because of its bitter taste, Soma is usually dropped into a victim's flavored drink. When Soma is metabolized into the victim's system, the body turns it into Meprobamate, a Schedule IV drug that is highly addictive.

On the Street

Soma is often sold at night clubs, raves, bars, schools, parties, and via the internet. Some dealers travel to Mexico to purchase the drug from illicit drug wholesalers, Mexican street dealers, or corrupt pharmacists. Dealers work social events to sell their drugs to predators and recreational abusers of the drug. Most Soma dealers sell other drugs to their customers. Predators can purchase their Soma, or other predatory drugs from a dealer far in advance or purchase the drug within hours or minutes of the assault. After the predator slips it into the unsuspecting victim's drink, Soma takes effect in 15 to 30 minutes and lasts for as long as 6 hours.

- **Technical name:** Carisoprodol
- **Controlled Substances Act Schedule:** Not sheduled
- **Classification:** Depressant
- **Appearance:** Soma is sold in a liquid or in a round oval tablet with 37 WALLACE imprinted on one side and Soma on the other. Other forms are diverted from pharmaceutical plants and corrupt pharmacists under the trade names Somadril, Carisoma, Artifar, Myolax, Caridolin, Chinchen, Flexartal, Neotica, Rela, Rotalin, Scutamil, Vanadom, Par 246, Somacid
- **Street names:** Soma, Par, Dees, Cid, Dance, Soma coma, Las Vegas Cocktail, 2001, 2403
- **Legal Uses:** Legally prescribed by doctors as a muscle relaxant and pain reliever for injuries.
- **Obvious Signs of Soma Use:** Giddy, relaxed, extremely relaxed, uncoordinated
- **Symptoms of Abuse:** Drowsy, nodding out, chills, headache, nausea, loss of coordination.

- **Risks of Abuse:** Depression, rapid heart rate, chest pains, insomnia, difficulty breathing, shock and death.
- **Addiction:** Psychologically addictive
- **Packaging:** Soma may be packaged on the street in a candy wrapper or package or commingled with other legal prescription drugs.
- **Paraphernalia:** Paraphernalia associated with Soma are eye droppers, pill crushers, small white paper envelopes, and small clear plastic Ziploc® bags.
- **Cutting Agents:** Often mixed with other drugs and dropped in alcoholic beverages or non alcoholic beverages.
- **Ingestion Methods:** Orally ingested by swallowing or drank in a drink.
- **Sought after Effects/High:** Relieve depression but as a predatory drug it is used to reach a relaxed state or sleep.
- **Street Prices:** *(based on the national average)*

    1 tablet sells for $5 to $25
    $135 to $1000 per 100 tablets on the internet

Other drugs used in predatory acts with much less frequency than GHB, Ketamine, Rohypnol, and Soma are Chloral Hydrate and Methaqualone: Chloral Hydrate is the drug that was originally notorious for its use in drug induced crimes during the 1940s through 1960s and depicted in many Hollywood movies exploiting its catchy street name of "Mickey Finn." It is the predecessor to today's predatory drugs. It is rarely encountered today but may be seen under the trade name Noctec. Methaqualone (Quaaludes) was extremely popular during the 1970s and 1980s during the "disco" era. Users were said to be "'luded out" because of their extremely drowsy state. It was often used during this era to commit drug assisted sexual assaults. Methaqualone is still used today for personal and criminal use but much less than GHB, Ketamine, Rohypnol, and Soma.

There are many other drugs that have been used in drug assisted sexual assault because of their similar effects on a person's body, especially when mixed with alcohol. These drugs are listed below under trade names and drug names: Ativan (Lorazepam) Dalmane (Flurazepam), Halcion (Triazolam), Klonopin or Rivotril (Clonazepam), Lexotan (Bromazepam), Librium (Chlordiazepoxide), Mogadon (Nitrazepam), ProSom (Estazolam), Restoril (Temazepam), Serax (Oxazepam), Valium (Diazepam), Versed (Midazolam), Xanax (Alprazolam), Ambien (Zolpidem Tartrate), Amytal (Amobarbitol), Equanil or Milltown (Meprobamate), Nembutol (Phenobarbitol), Placidyl (Ethchlorvynol), Seconal (Secobarbitol), Benedryl (Diphenhydramine), Flexeril (Cyclobenzaprine), Telazol (Tiletamine/Zolazepam), Transderm Scop (Scopolamine), Paral (Paraldehyde), Doriden (Gluthethimide), Quaalude or Sopor (Methaqualone).

Inhalants

Inhalants used for getting high

In 1981, I was a young patrol officer when I first came in contact with a crazed criminal under the influence of an inhalant. For several hours, this "Go" head, as he was called on the streets, committed 25 separate crimes until I was able to catch him before he killed anyone, and himself. He was under the influence of, what was commonly called on the street "Go" fluid. "Go" fluid was transmission fluid and this maniac was inhaling it regularly. After trying to kill several people with his car, causing multiple accidents, assaulting several people, robbing someone, shooting at others and trying to kill me, I was able to apprehend him and wrestle him to the ground with the help of several back-up officers.

"Go" fluid made him go wild. It causes the brain to short circuit and, caused permanent damage. "Go" fluid was just one of many products and chemicals regularly abused by people in this country every day.

Inhalants, which are often a free or cheap high, became popular in the 1950s when teenagers starting glue sniffing. Glue sniffing grew into inhaled abuse of a variety of substances. The most common types of inhalants today, abused in the U.S., are aerosol sprays, glue, spray paint, solvents, and gases. These inhalants are usually sniffed, snorted, bagged, or huffed. The most frightening thing about inhalants is that grammar school and high school aged children are the biggest abusers.

The products and chemicals abused as inhalants cover a wide range of household products. Here are some that are frequently abused:

- **Nitrites:** Chemicals, such as amyl nitrite and butyl nitrite, are abused for the purpose of enhancing sexual experience. Amyl nitrite usually can be found in small sealed capsules that are popped open to release the vapors. They are called "Poppers" on the street. They are often purchased at adult bookstores or the internet. Butyl Nitrate is sold in small bottles and also called poppers.
- **Solvents:** Solvents are liquid chemicals that have a strong odor and produce vapors that are irritating and harmful. Solvents can be in paint thinner,

gasoline, correction fluid, felt-tip markers, nail polish, nail polish remover, glue.
- **Aerosols:** These are sprays that have propellants to forcibly emit the solvent from the can. One of the most common solvents found in aerosols is toluene. Aerosols include spray paint, deodorant, hair spray, cooking spray, fabric protector and static remover.
- **Gases:** Gases include products such as whipped cream, air conditioning units, butane lighters and nitrous oxide (laughing gas). Nitrous oxide is common at the rave parties and the club scene. They are often stolen from dentist's offices. Other products that contain nitrous oxide are "whippets" which are whip cream canister cartridges for reusable dispensers sold in gourmet food stores and found in restaurants.

- **Street Names:** Amys, Bang, bolt, Boppers, Bullet, Climax, Glading, Gluey, Hardware, Head Cleaner, Hippie Crack, Huff, kick, Locker Room, Poor Man's Pot, Poppers, Rush, Snappers, Toncho
- **Ingestion Methods:** Sniffing is the short breathing of fumes from a chemical substance, such as a marker or glue but can be breathed in a bag with the inhalant at the bottom. Huffing is the inhaling of fumes from of rag soaked with the inhalant.

- **Snorting:** Inhaling the fumes of a chemical deeply and holding the fumes in your lungs for several seconds before exhaling.
- **Obvious Signs of Inhalant Use:** Dizzy, Drunk, Vomiting, Odor of chemicals from clothing or on skin, Runny Nose, Nausea, Lethargic
- **Symptoms of Abuse:** Hallucinations, Brain Damage, Hearing Loss, Blindness, Heart and Lung Problems, Kidney Damage, Liver Damage, Death
- **Risks of Addiction:** Addictive
- **Sought After Effects/High:** Rapid Euphoric Affect, similar to alcohol consumption followed by excitation, drowsiness and lightheadedness. Nitrous oxide users seek to enhance sexual experiences.

Prescription Drugs

The term used to describe the illegal sale of prescription drugs is called diversion. Diversion can occur by many means, including, but not limited to corrupt pharmacists, theft of drugs by other medical professionals and workers, unscrupulous people who go doctor shopping (obtain multiple prescriptions for the same drug), theft from family or friends, and acquiring drugs through fraudulent prescriptions. These methods supply the illicit prescription drug dealer and abusers.

The National Household survey on Drug Abuse indicates that an estimated 36 million people in the U.S. ages 12 and older abused prescription drugs once in their lifetime. The survey also stated that millions of teenagers and adults abuse prescription drugs regularly. Prescription drug abuse among high school students, according to the University of Michigan's Monitoring the Future Survey, is at an alarming rate over 10%. These drugs are administered orally, through skin patches, or injected, but maybe available in suppositories. When these drugs are abused, they are usually snorted, smoked, injected, taken orally or skin-popped.

A recent frightening diversion of prescription drugs by teenagers, occurring across the U.S., is called a "Grab Bag Party." The Grab Bag Party is a party involving teenagers who steal prescription drugs and over the counter drugs from their parent's medicine cabinets and each teenager places the drugs in a pile and they grab whatever they can and get high with the drugs. These teenagers don't even know what they are taking.

Prescription drugs, commonly abused in the U.S., can be placed in three categories: (1) Narcotics, Opioids, and Pain Relievers (2) Depressants and (3) Stimulants.

In the tables that follow, the "Street Name" column has been left blank so that you can fill in the street name that is common in your own area.

Narcotics/Opioids/Pain Relievers

The drugs in this category, generally are prescribed for pain relief, cough suppression, diarrhea, and induce anesthesia. They produce a feeling of well being because of their ability to reduce pain, anxiety, and depression. Frequently abused drugs in this category are listed in the chart below.

Trade Name	Drug	Street Name
Codeine	codeine	
Darvon	propoxyphene	
Dilaudid	hydromorphone	
Demerol	meperedine	
Darvocet	propoxyphene	
Fentanyl		
Lorcet	hydrocodone	
Lortab	hydrocodone	
Methadone	Methadone	

Trade Name	Drug	Street Name
Ms-Contin	oxycodone	
MSIR	oxycodone	
Morphine	morphine	
Oramorph	oxycodone	
Oxycodone	oxycodone	
Oxycontin	oxycodone	
Percocet	oxycodone	
Percodan	oxycodone	
RMS	oxycodone	
Thebaine	thebaine	
Tylenol #2, #3, #4	codeine	
Vicodin	hydrocodone	

Obvious Signs of Use: Impaired coordination, drowsy, confused, dilated pupils, fatigue

Symptoms of Abuse: Low Heart Rate, Low Blood Pressure, impaired memory, nightmares, tremors

Risks of Abuse: Physical and psychological dependence
Risks of Addiction: Highly addictive
Street Prices: $5 to $20 per tablet

Depressants

Depressants are prescribed for the treatment of anxiety, sleep disorders, muscle relaxation, epilepsy, stress, and convulsions. The abuse of depressants is increasing, especially among 12 to 17 year olds. Depressants can make the user relaxed, sleepy, and lethargic.

Trade Name	Chemical	Street Name
Ativan	lorazepam	
Ambien	zolpidem	
Diazephan	diazepam	
Klonopin	clonazepam	
Quaalude	methaqualone	
Librium	chlordiazepoxide	
Methadone	buprenorphine	

Trade Name	Chemical	Street Name
Milltown	meprobamate	
Seconal	secobarbitol	
Sonata		
Tuinal	secobarbitol	
Valium	diazepam	
Xanax	alprazolam	
Xyrem		

- **Obvious Signs of Use:** Poor coordination, lethargy, sleepy
- **Symptoms of Abuse:** Low Blood Pressure, Low Heart Rate, Impaired Memory, Nightmares
- **Long Term Risks of Abuse:** Tremors, Amnesia, Loss of Muscle Control
- **Risks of Addiction:** Highly Addictive
- **Street Prices:** $3 to $10 per tablet

Stimulants

Stimulants affect the Central Nervous System and are used to treat ADD (Attention Deficit Disorder) and ADHD (Attention Deficit Hyperactivity Disorder), Narcolepsy, Weight Control, Appetite.

Trade Name	Chemical	Street Name
Adderall	Amphetamine	
Adipex	Phentermine	
Biphetamine *Dexi*	Amphetamin & Dextroamphetmine	
Dexedrine *Dexi*	Dextroamphetmine	
Lonamin	Phentermine	
Prelu	Phendimetrazine	
Pseudoephedrine		
Ritalin *Vitamin R*	Methylphenidate	

- **Obvious Signs of Use:** Hyperactive, jittery, highly alert, aggressive.
- **Symptoms of Abuse:** Bloodshot eyes, dilated pupils
- **Risks of Abuse:** High blood pressure, hypertension, stroke, heart attack.
- **Risks of Addiction:** Highly addictive
- **Street Prices:** $5 to $10 per tablet

Anabolic Steroids

Anabolic steroids include testosterone, the male hormone found in humans (male and female) and many synthetic steroids called anabolic-androgenic steroids. Anabolic steroids have many legal medical uses, such as breast cancer treatment, anemia treatment, and impotence treatment. There are several types of these anabolic steroids sold legally in the U.S. for health purposes as well as veterinary use.

Scientists studied steroid use in Germany from the 1800's to the 1930's. In the mid 1900's, steroids were used to enhance an athletes performance and growth. This phenomenon made international attention when the Soviet Union Weight Lifting Team and other athletes were discovered to be using testosterone which enhanced their size, strength and performance contributing to their great success.

In the U.S., steroids were developed in 1956 by Dr. John Zieglar, who was a U.S. Olympic Team Physician, after discovering the Soviets use of steroids. Steroid use became common, although covert, in athletes until 1990 when Congress passed a law (Anabolic Steroids Control Act) which placed Anabolic Steroids on the Controlled Substances Act as a Schedule III Substance.

Most Anabolic Steroids sold on the illicit market today come from foreign suppliers. As in other illegal substances destined for the U.S., Mexico is the leading supplier. The large majority of steroid abusers in the U.S. are athletes and weight lifters who are purchasing counterfeit steroids or steroids manufactured with harmful substances.

On The Street

Most steroid sales are confined to dealers who hang out at competitions, gyms, health clubs, college campuses, high schools, and some sales via the mail or the internet. The most commonly encountered steroids sold on the street are Testosterone, Nandrolone, Methenolone, Stanozolol, Methandrostenolone, Boldenone, Fluxoymesterone, Methandroil, Methyl testosterone, Oxandrolone, Oxymetholone, Andriol, Danatrol, Orabolin, Sustanon:

- **Obvious Signs of Use:** Rapid muscle growth, weight gain, increased strength, aggression, erectile and sexual dysfunction, voice changes.
- **Symptoms of Abuse:** Aggressive, loss of hair, irritable.

- **Risks of Abuse:** Hypertension, high blood pressure, stroke, heart attack.
- **Risks of Addiction:** Addictive
- **Street Prices:** based on national average

Andriol:	$1 for a 40 mg capsule
Danatrol:	$2 to $3 for a 200 mg capsule
Methyltestosterone:	$1 for Two 50 mg tablets
Orabolin:	$1 to $2 for a 20 mg capsule
Sustanon:	$10 to $30 per ml

Plant Drugs

There are plants that are indigenous to specific regions across the world that are often abused in the U.S. These drugs that are abused less frequently from the others mentioned in the previous sections but they, undoubtedly deserve a mention in this pocketguide because they are also sold on the street and can be a major problem in specific areas across the U.S. These drugs are Salvia Divinorum, Khat, Mushrooms, and Peyote.

Salvia Divinorum

Salvia Divinorum, or Salvia D, is a plant that contains the drug Salvinorin A which is a psychoactive substance with similar properties to Marijuana. According to law enforcement sources, Salvia D has been turning up in the

Northeast, Midwest, and Pacific regions of the U.S. but extremely high in Missouri. Salvia D and Salvinorin A are ***not currently scheduled*** by the federal government but has been locally regulated in the city of St Peters, Missouri, because of the high rates of abuse by adolescents. St Peters residents enacted a local ordinance in January 2003 to regulate the distribution of Salvia D. The ordinance, makes it "unlawful for any person to engage in the sale or distribution of Salvia D, aka Salvinorin A, or any variation thereof, to any individual who is 17 years of age or younger."

Salvia D, also called Salvia, Sal D, Ska Maria Pastora, SMP, Sage, Diviner's Sage, Sage of Seers, produces debilitating hallucinations with prolonged abuse. Users report the effects as an experience in time travel or loss of concern about time, becoming in touch with inanimate objects, and psychedelic trips. Salvia D is a green leafy plant with square hollow stems that grows up to heights of three feet or more. The plant grows in large clusters and has large bright green leaves with purple and white flowers. The leaves of the plant are dried and smoked or brewed in a tea in its fresh state. The leaves can also be placed between the teeth and gums and chewed like chewing tobacco. Occasionally, Salvia D is converted into a liquid and vaporized for inhalation ingestion. Salvia D is sold at head shops, over the internet, and via mail deliveries but can be grown locally. It sells for $15 to $120 per ounce of leaves but the liquid extract is sold for $110 to $300 per ounce.

Khat

Khat, pronounced "cot," is a flowering plant native to northeastern Africa (Somalia) and the Arabian peninsula (Yemen). Khat is a green shrub that has purple-ish stems with green leaves similar to a mint leaf. Khat leaves are chewed, similar to tobacco, causing an ingestion of its active ingredient, Cathinone. The Cathinone causes a mild amphetamine-like feeing similar to methamphetamine or cocaine. Khat is ingested in its fresh state which is 48 hours from being cut from the plant since it's potency deteriorates rapidly. In its fresh state, Khat is a Schedule I controlled substance but after a few days, unless refrigerated, it can have diminished potency to a Schedule IV controlled substance.

Khat, which is chewed, brewed in a tea, or smoked in a "Shisha" Pipe, causes insomnia, mild depression, hyperactivity, and loss of appetite. It has been reported to cause damage to the Central Nervous System, Circulatory System, Respiratory System, Circulatory System, and Digestive System.

Khat, is also called Cot, Cat, Abyssian Tea, African Tea, Arab Tea, Bushman's Tea, Chat, Gat, Got, Kat, Miraa, Oat, Qat, Quat, Somali Tea, Tohai, and Tschat. It has been referred to on the streets as "Black Hawk Down" because it was ingested by Somali fighters in the battle with U.S. troops in Mogadishu to enhance their fighting ability. This fact was highlighted in the movie, Black Hawk Down. Khat has also been linked to terrorist groups operating across the U.S., especially, in NY, Detroit, and London and is a funding source for these terrorist groups.

Khat abuse is high in regions across the U.S. with sizable Arabic and Somali populations, such as New York, Los Angeles, Detroit, Dearborn, Boston, Minneapolis/St Paul, Nashville, Paterson and Jersey City, and similar cities. In these areas, the pervasive abuse of Khat enables the user to work long hours without sleep.

- **Street Prices:** *(based on the national average)*

    Khat is generally sold in bundles (of leaves) that sell for $35 to $50 per bundle.

Mushrooms

Mushrooms have been used to acquire a "high" for centuries. They have been used by Indian cultures as part of their rituals, in Mexico and Central America. Mushrooms became popular during the 1960s in the U.S. and became known as "Magic Mushrooms" because of their hallucinogenic effects. Mushrooms are also called Halo, Shrooms, Wild Mushrooms, and Food of the Gods. They contain two substances regulated by the Controlled Substance Act as a Schedule I. The substances, Psilocybin and Psilocin are contained in over one hundred different species of mushrooms. The psychoactive substances in the Psilocybin mushrooms, Psilocybin, is identified as phosphorylated 4-hydroxymethyltryptamine. In Psilocin, the chemical is identified as 4-hydroxydimethyltryptamine.

Mushrooms containing Psilocybin and Psilocin grow wild throughout the U.S., especially in the western and southern regions. Mushrooms are grown in illicit labs or personal gardens across the U.S., but most of the supply abused in the U.S. are smuggled in from Mexico, Central America, or purchased on the internet. Another form of mushrooms used to get "high" is called the Amanita Mushroom. Unlike the Psilocybin Mushrooms, the Amanita Mushrooms contain Mucimol and Ibutonic Acid which are not controlled substances, thus they are available for sale through mail order, via the internet, and at rogue health food suppliers. Amenita Mushrooms grow wild across the U.S. and can be identified by their brown, red, yellow, or orange caps with white leaves.

Mushrooms are usually sold in plastic bags to preserve their potency. The mushrooms are often sold dried, in pieces, or in a powder form and sold in capsules or in paper envelopes. Mushrooms are purchased to provide the user with a trip similar to LSD or mescaline. Abusers of Mushrooms will have pupil dilation, flushed face, slurred speech, dizziness, twitching, and blinking. The results of abuse can be blurred vision, light-headedness, shivering, stomach pains, nausea, hallucinations, psychosis, mood swings, and panic attacks. Mushrroms are psychologically addictive.

- **Street Prices:** *(based on the national average)*

    1 dose is usually 20mg to 50 mg that sells for $10 to $25
    ¼ ounce sells for $25 to $100
    1 ounce sells for $100 to $150
    ¼ lb sells for $175 to $250
    1 lb sells for $300 to $1500

Peyote

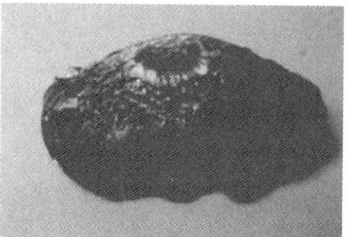

Peyote with the crown (button)

Peyote is a cactus species known as Lophophora Williamsii Lemaire that grows in northern Mexico and southern Texas. Peyote Cactus has an active ingredient, commonly known as Mescaline. Mescaline is identified as 3, 45-trimethoxyphenethylamine. Peyote is described as a cactus with no spines and a "crown" or "button" on top that is dried and ground to sell on the illicit market. Peyote is a hallucinogenic that can be psychologically addictive for the user. Peyote is abused for a feeling of an alcohol-like high and to reach a "feel good" state.

Peyote can be chewed or soaked in water or tea to create an intoxicating drink. Users of Peyote can have dilated pupils, slurred speech, unsteady gait, and may be sweating and confused. Hallucinations, and elevated heart rate and blood pressure can result. Peyote is sold in small clear plastic Ziploc® bags or small paper envelopes. Peyote is also called Pey, Buttons, Crowns, Caps, Chief, Dry whiskey, Green whiskey, Hikuri, Mesc, Mescal, Mescaline, Nubs, Top, Tops, Seni, and Britton.

- **Street Prices:** *(based on the national average)*

    1 "crown" (or button) sells for $5 to $20
    1 gram sells for $25 to $100

Over the Counter Drugs

Over the counter drugs, legally sold in drug stores, supermarkets, and convenience stores all over the United States are also frequently abused and can cause adverse effects when ingested outside the recommended dosages. One such Over The Counter (OTC) drug is Dextromethorphan, also known as DXM. It is available in many OTC products used for cough suppression and treatment of cold symptoms. DXM comes in liquid, lozenges, tablets, capsules, and gel caps. DXM can be developed into a powder by extracting the drug from cough syrup. Once the powder is extracted it can be pressed into tablets and is often sold on the street as ecstasy. DXM, in its powder form, can be snorted.

DXM can be legally purchased in stores, on the internet, or stolen from home medicine cabinets, stores, or diverted by corrupt pharmacists or medical employees. The majority of DXM abusers are teenagers. Other DXM abusers are those individuals who are looking for a quick "high" when the preferred drug is unavailable. Typical forms of DXM abuse include "Robo Shakes" which is the drinking of a large amount of cough syrup containing DXM followed by a forced vomit in order to absorb the DXM throughout the abuser's stomach lining. DXM abusers also create a "DXM Cocktail" which is a mixture of cough syrup and 7-Up (or other carbonated drink). The carbonation enhances the effects of the DXM in the stomach, rather than vomiting.

DXM abusers have many street names. The street names for DXM are Dex, Drex, Dextro, DM, Syrup, Robo, Rojo, Triple C, CeCeCe, Cori, Red Devils, Skittles, Tuss, and Velvet. Some DXM abusers either purchase tablets over the internet and take them orally or crush the tablets and snort them. Some, who extract the powder from liquid cough syrup, are known to snort the powder while others will soak a cigarette or marijuana cigarette into a bottle of cough syrup and smoke it.

Abusers of DXM, and other OTC medications, experience a high, known as plateaus. These plateaus occur in four stages. These stages are (1) Slight intoxication (2) Intoxication similar to alcohol with mild hallucinations (3) Sensory impairment (4) An out of body experience resulting in the loss of contact with the senses. These abusers are seeking a high similar to that of PCP (Phencyclidine) which can bring on intoxication, mild hallucinations, and an out of body-type experience. Abuse of the drug can result in slurred speech, memory loss, impaired coordination and vision, as well as hypertension, fever, itching, sweating, and a potential fro coma.

DXM tablets are sold at raves, middle schools, high schools, and college campuses. Some tablets appear as colored tablets and often in the shape of a cross, or tabkets with an icon or logo embossed on the face.

Some OTC medications that contain DXM are Robitussin® Cough Syrup, Robitussin® Cold and Congestion, Best Tussin Cough Suppression, Coricidin® HBP Cough and Cold, and Alka Seltxer Plus Cold and Cough Medicine. There are also many store brands of these products that are widely sold containing DXM and other abused drugs. These other commonly abused drugs are Acetaminophen (pain reliever), Ephedrine and Pseudoephedrine (stimulant), Guaifenesin (expectorant), and Chlorpheniramine (Maleate (antihistamine).

- **Street Prices:** *(based on the national average)*

    1 DXM tablet sells for $5 to $10 but is often sold to unsuspecting users as Ecstasy for much higher.

Bibliography

The following trusted sources, as well as personal interviews with some of the Nation's best narcotics investigators, have resulted n the ground-breaking information in this book.

1. Drugs of Abuse: Drug Enforcement Administration
2. National Drug Intelligence Center
3. Drug Identification Bible (2006 Edition) Ameri-Chem
4. Cocaine Fast Facts: NDIC
5. Crack Fast Facts: NDIC
6. Heroin Fast Facts: NDIC
7. MDMA Fast Facts: NDIC
8. Methamphetamine Fast Facts: NDIC
9. Office of Narcotics and Drug Control Policy (ONDCP)
10. Mid-Atlantic Great Lakes Organized Crime Law Enforcement Network
11. NYPD Narcotics Division Manual
12. Illegal Drugs: *A Complete Guide to Their History, Chemistry, Use & Abuse* by Paul Gahlinger

Glossary

8 ball	Eighth of an ounce
Amphetamine	A drug that is a stimulant.
BC Bud	Canadian produced marijuana
Bindle	A bag
Boat	1,000 tablets
Bongs	Smoking device, usually a large pipe used to smoke or inhale drugs that are smoked
Bottled Water	Used to dilute drugs like GHB, Ketamine, and other drugs that are water soluble; Used to drink when under the influence of Ecstasy because of raised body temperature.
Bundle	10 bags
Chip	1 gram
CG	Commercial Grade

Crack pipe	Five inch glass tube used to smoke crack; Also called a stem.
Dip	To dip a cigarette or joint into a drug liquid such as PCP, or Formaldehyde.
Dose	one serving; one hit
DU	Dosage Unit
g	gram
Glassine Envelopes	Small thin paper envelopes that are slightly transparent and wax-like that are used to contain small amounts of powdered drugs such as heroin, cocaine, and others.
Hallucination	Seeing things that are not present. Usually brought about when a person is under the influence of a psychoactive drug. is a sensory perception experienced in the absence of an external stimulus, as distinct from an illusion, which is a misperception of an external stimulus. Hallucinations may occur

	in any sensory modality - visual, auditory, olfactory, gustatory, tactile, or proprioceptive (sense of balance and position in space).
Hallucinogenic	A drug capable of causing hallucinations.
HIV/AIDS	Human Immunodeficiency Virus / Acquired Immune Deficiency Syndrome
HIDTA	High Intensity Drug Trafficking Area
High	The feeling that drug abusers seek from ingesting drugs. A high can range from a immediate stimulation or rush, to a euphoric effect and a sensory impairment; Intoxication.
hit	One toke on a joint; one serving of drug
Hydro	Hydroponic marijuana
Ice	ICE-Methamphetamine: Crystalline form of meth.

Illusion	a distortion of a sensory perception, Disambiguation
Inhalants	Common household items containing chemicals, or any item that are abused by inhaling the fumes, vapors, or chemicals.
Inhalers	Nasal tubes used to inhale a antihistamine or other substance.
Intramuscular	Into the muscle; A coomon way of injecting the drug with a hypodermic.
Intravenous	Into the vein; A common way of injecting a drug with a hypodermic.
Jar	100 tablets
kg	kilogram
lb	pound
mcg	microgram
mg	milligram

Mickey Finn	a slang term for a drug-laced drink given to someone without their knowledge in order to incapacitate them. Serving someone a Mickey Finn is most commonly referred to as "slipping a mickey."
ml	milliliter
NDIC	National Drug Intelligence Center
Nodding out	Starting to fall asleep; Head nods downward until consciousness and then it happens again.
ONDCP	Office of National Drug Control Policy
Oz	ounce
Pacifiers	Baby pacifiers, plastic nipples, or candy pacifiers used, usually with Ecstasy, to safeguard from teeth grinding brought about by the use of the drug.
Paper	¼ gram

Paper envelopes	Small envelopes, usually Pyramid Papers, used to contain small amounts of powdered drugs.
Piece	25 grams
Plastic Bag(gies)	Small clear plastic sandwich sized bags.
Precursors	Any substance used to create a drug or mix with a drug.
Pop	Short for "Skin pop"; A method of inserting a drug under the skin, usually into a self inflicted cut of laceration.
Pyramid Paper	A strong paper square used to contain a drug powder or other valuable item by folding it into an envelope.
Rack	To steal something.
Roach clips	an alligator clip, usually an electronic clip, used to hold a burning joint to avoid burning the fingertips.

Rolling Paper	Thin papers used to roll marijuana into a cigarette or tobacco.
Rubber Stamps	A rubber inked stamp used to ink a trademark or brand on a package of drugs.
Rush	A feeling of a drug taking effect on the abuser.
Scent Masking Agents	Air fresheners, coffee, eucalyptus, menthol or any substance with a strong scent used to cover the scent of drugs with a discernable odor.
Shisha	A water pipe usually found in Middle Eastern cultures used to smoke tobacco, hash, or other substances.
Shooting Gallery	A place, usually a house or abandoned building, used for intravenous drug users to "shoot up" (inject) their drugs.
Sift	To strain drugs in a screen or device used to crush drugs to a fine powder.

Skin Pop	To insert drugs, usually powder or tablets, into a cut in the skin (usually self inflicted) for the purpose of ingesting the drug and getting "high."
Snort(ing)	To inhale a powder or substance into one nasal passage at a time as an ingestion method.
Speedball	An injection of heron and cocaine mixed.
Stacking	Taking two drugs at the same time.
Tin Foil	Aluminum foil torn into small pieces used to contain drugs.
Vials	Clear Glass or Clear plastic tubes or small jars used to contain powdered or liquid drugs.
Wet	A cigarette or joint soaked in liquid PCP or Formaldehyde.
Wet dance	A drunken stupor involving foot movements, jokingly called a dance by someone under the influence of "wet."

Works　　　　　　　　Paraphernalia used to ingest a drug; More commonly refers to paraphernalia used to inject Heroin. Works include a hypodermic syringe, metal spoon or metal bottle cap, a lighter or matches, and a cotton ball or cigarette filter.

Ziploc® bags　　　　　Ziploc® bags are common household clear plastic bags used to contain a food or substance. Some Ziploc® bags range in size from small (½ inch by ½ inch to several inches) to large (Several inches to 12 or more inches in width). Ziploc® bags are frequently used to contain drugs.

NOTES

NOTES

Field Testing Made Easier with IDenta Drug and Explosive ID Kits

Field Test Meth. X, Crack, Coke, Hash, Heroin, and even explosives in minutes!

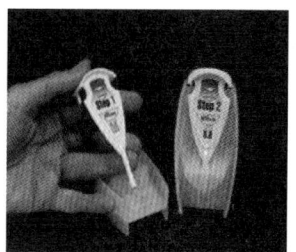 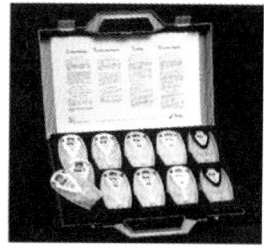

IDenta Drug testing kits are sold by AquilaVision, a company that is owned and operated by cops providing products for cops. IDenta Drug and Explosive Identification Kits test substances for the chemical properties of a suspected illegal narcotics or suspected explosive. Our drug identification test kits are currently sold in the U.S. and many other countries throughout the world. Currently, the IDenta kits are being used by U.S. Department of State, D.E.A., and many local, and state law enforcement agencies. IDenta's test kits are safer, more reliable, more cost effective, and far superior than other kits.

IDenta is currently the ONLY DRUG IDENTIFICATION KIT on the market that ELIMINATES ALL KNOWN FALSE POSITIVES when testing suspected Illegal Drugs. This is important because it means a savings of Officer's time, Prosecutor's time, Product loss cost, Lab Time and testing costs resulting from False Positives an officer may receive in the field. Officer safety is paramount, and with our hard plastic casing, we drastically reduce the possibility of injury to the user.

IDenta Drug Identification kits are the only Field Test Kits that, due to their unique design, can test drug paraphernalia for residue of illegal narcotics. We have also included in each of our test kits, an "Acid-Neutralizer" ampoule that when broken, mixes with the active chemical reagents to ensure the product safety for proper disposal. Our competitors make you pay extra for this feature.

Find out why law-enforcement agencies are saying IDenta drug testing kits are the drug testing product of choice!

Contact:

Sheriff Bill Slaughter
Director of Public Safety Solutions
1121 E. Broadway Suite 105, Missoula Montana 59802
bslaughter@aquilavision.com , www.aquilavision.com
406-532-3260 office, 406-396-7208 cell

Homefront Protective Group's Most Popular Law Enforcement Training Programs

- ✓ StreetCop Tactics™
- ✓ Counter Terrorism for Local Law Enforcement
- ✓ Identity Theft: Interdiction and Investigation
- ✓ Innovative Crime Fighting Strategies
- ✓ Tactical Prisoner Debriefing Method
- ✓ Proactive Gang Interdiction and Intelligence
- ✓ PROACTIVE Interdiction
- ✓ Counter Terrorism for Local Law Enforcement
- ✓ Hidden Compartments and Drug Stashes

For information on our dynamic training seminars contact us at 877-232-7500, email us at

homefrontprotect@aol.com

or visit our website at

www.homefrontprotect.com

Other Pocketguides by Lou Savelli
Available Through Looseleaf Law Publications

Basic Crime Scene Investigation $9.95

Gangs 9.95

Graffiti 9.95

Proactive Law Enforcement Guide for the War on Terror 9.95

Identity Theft 9.95

Cop Jokes 9.95

Practical Spanish for Law Enforcement Officers ... 9.95

**For a complete list of all Looseleaf Law publications
call for a free catalog or visit our website**

(800) 647-5547   www.LooseleafLaw.com

OTHER TITLES OF INTEREST
FROM LOOSELEAF LAW PUBLICATIONS, INC.

Real World Search & Seizure
 A Street Handbook for Law Enforcement
 by Matthew J. Medina

Anatomy of a Motor Vehicle Stop
 Essentials of Safe Traffic Enforcement
 by Joseph & Matthew Petrocelli

Advanced Vehicle Stop Tactics
 Skills for Today's Survival Conscious Officer
 by Michael T. Rayburn

Advanced Patrol Tactics
 Skills for Today's Street Cop
 by Michael T. Rayburn

Building a Successful Law Enforcement Career
 Common Sense Wisdom for the New Officer
 by Ryan E. Melsky, M.A., J.D.

How to Really, *Really* Write Those Boring Police Reports
 by Kimberly Clark

Use of Force
 Expert Guidance for Decisive Force Response
 by Brian A. Kinnaird

(800) 647-5547 www.LooseleafLaw.com